Bulletin Boards That Kids Make and Do
Contents

D1609118

Introduction

This all-in-one resource helps meet teachers' need for child-created and interactive teaching bulletin boards.

- Bulletin boards target state and national learning **standards**.
- Bulletin board ideas are organized by **content areas**.
- 40 **skills** are targeted.

  12 language arts   8 science
  12 math   8 social studies

- 3 bulletin board ideas for each skill have varying levels of student difficulty: ✂ easy, ✂✂ medium, ✂✂✂ hard.
- Bulletin board ideas for classroom management showcase student work and good behavior.
- 40 color **photographs** show completed bulletin boards.
- Detailed **instructions** are included for teachers and students.
- 100 pages of reproducible **patterns** add to your bulletin board library.
- **Online resources**, too!

  20-plus additional bulletin board ideas at www.harcourtachieve.com/achievementzone

200 plus bulletin board ideas make learning fun!

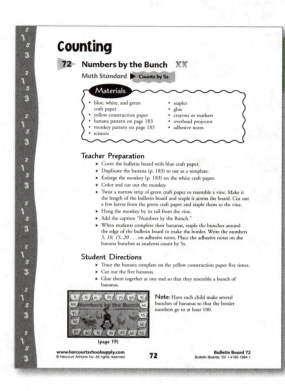

Illustrated Bulletin Board Page

- Skill
- Bulletin Board Title
- Difficulty Level
- Standard
- Materials List
- Teacher Preparation
- Student Directions
- Reduced Illustration

Two Additional Ideas for Each Main Bulletin Board Skill

- Bulletin Board Title
- Difficulty Level
- Standard
- Instructions

Use the same basic bulletin board materials, but expand into two different boards!

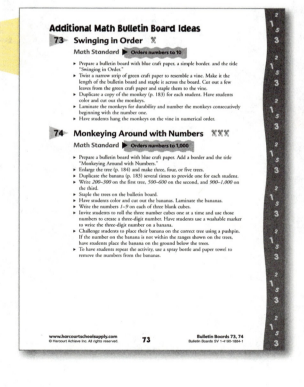

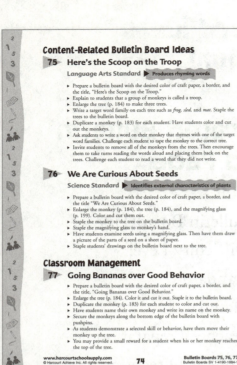

Three additional pattern-related bulletin boards for a variety of content areas and/or for classroom management.

Convenient, Easy-to-Use Indexes

- Standards (pp. 5–8)
- Skills (pp. 9–12)
- Patterns (pp. 153–253)

Language Arts Standards

Mathematics Standards

Science Standards

Social Studies Standards

Bulletin Boards, SV 1-4190-1884-1

Skill Index

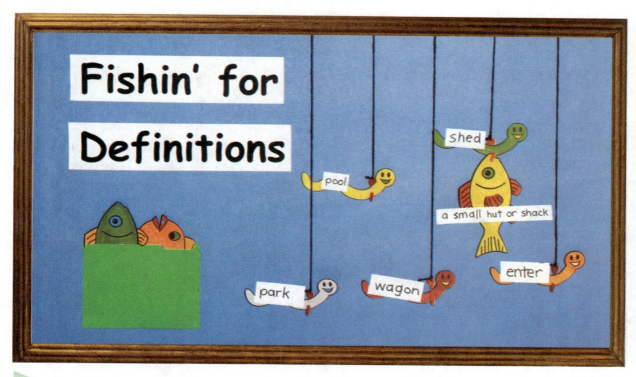

1 ▶ Alphabet

See page 33 for materials list and directions.

7 ▶ Genres

See page 36 for materials list and directions.

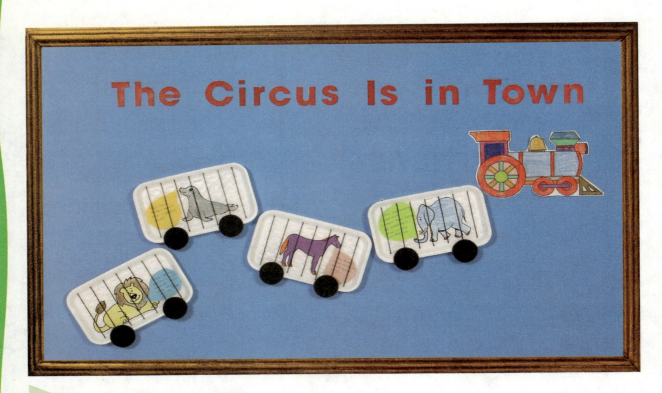

12 Grammar

See page 39 for materials list and directions.

17 Parts of a Book

See page 42 for materials list and directions.

22 ▶ Phonics

See page 45 for materials list and directions.

28 ▶ Punctuation

See page 48 for materials list and directions.

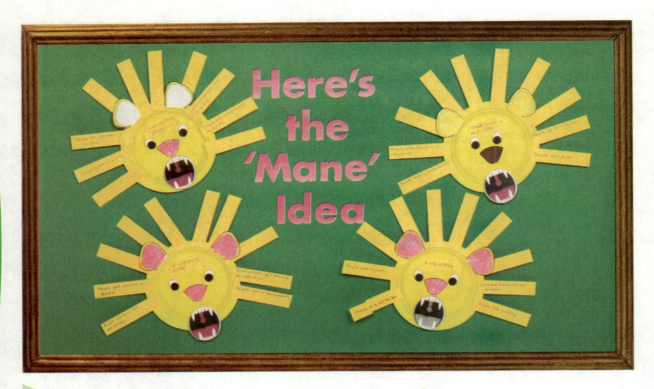

33 Reading Comprehension

See page 51 for materials list and directions.

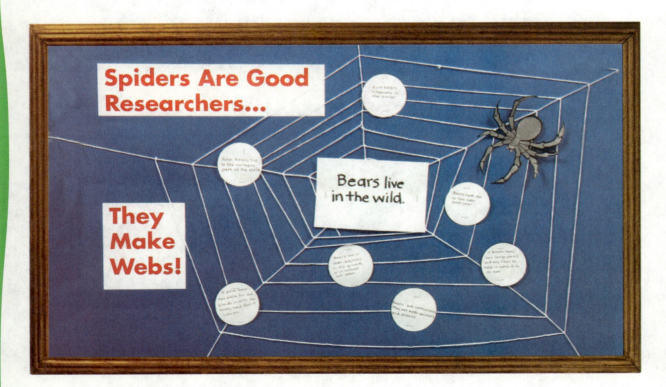

38 Research

See page 54 for materials list and directions.

43 ▶ Rhyming Words

See page 57 for materials list and directions.

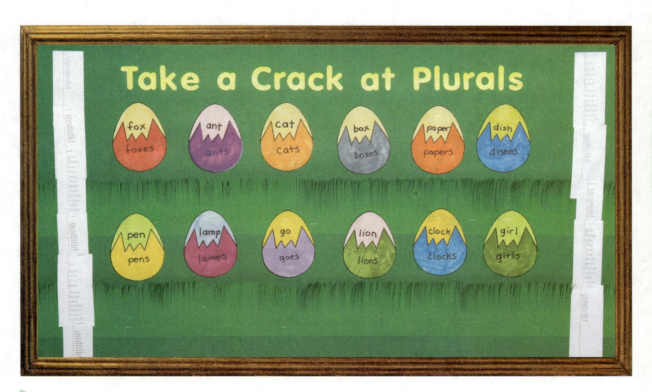

49 ▶ Spelling

See page 60 for materials list and directions.

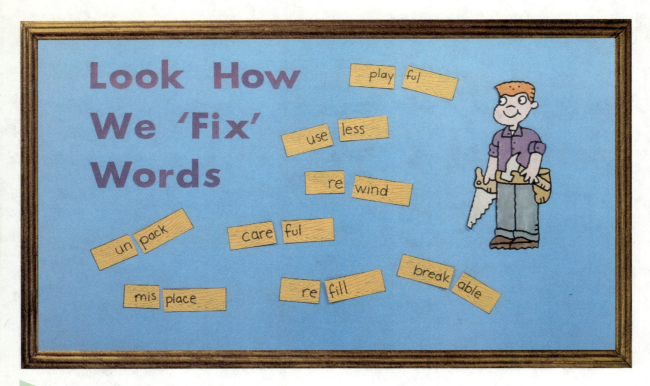

55 ▶ **Vocabulary**

See page 63 for materials list and directions.

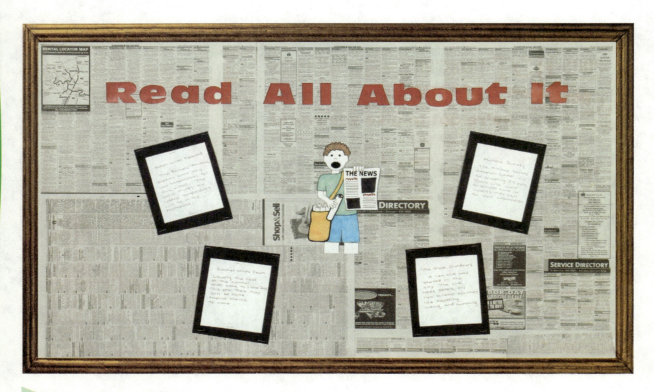

60 ▶ **Writing Process**

See page 66 for materials list and directions.

66 ▸ Computation

See page 69 for materials list and directions.

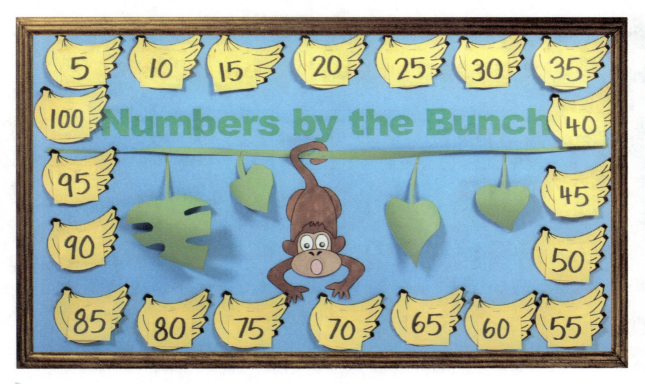

72 ▸ Counting

See page 72 for materials list and directions.

78 Fractions

See page 75 for materials list and directions.

83 Graphs

See page 78 for materials list and directions.

88 ▶ **Measurement**

See page 81 for materials list and directions.

93 ▶ **Money**

See page 84 for materials list and directions.

98 Patterns

See page 87 for materials list and directions.

103 Probability

See page 90 for materials list and directions.

109 Problem Solving

See page 93 for materials list and directions.

115 Shapes

See page 96 for materials list and directions.

121 Sorting and Classifying

See page 99 for materials list and directions.

126 Time

See page 102 for materials list and directions.

131 Animals

See page 105 for materials list and directions.

137 Environment

See page 108 for materials list and directions.

143 Nutrition

See page 111 for materials list and directions.

148 Plants

See page 114 for materials list and directions.

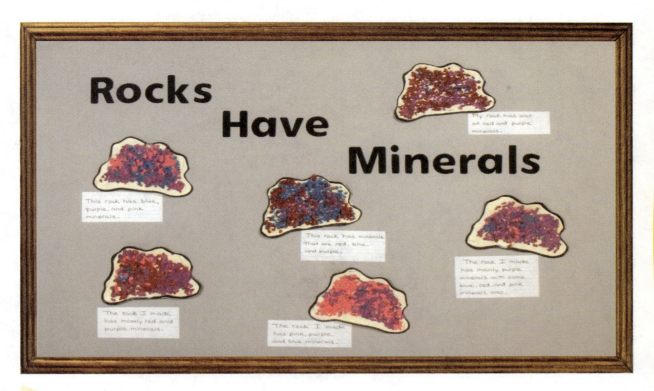

153 Rocks

See page 117 for materials list and directions.

159 Safety

See page 120 for materials list and directions.

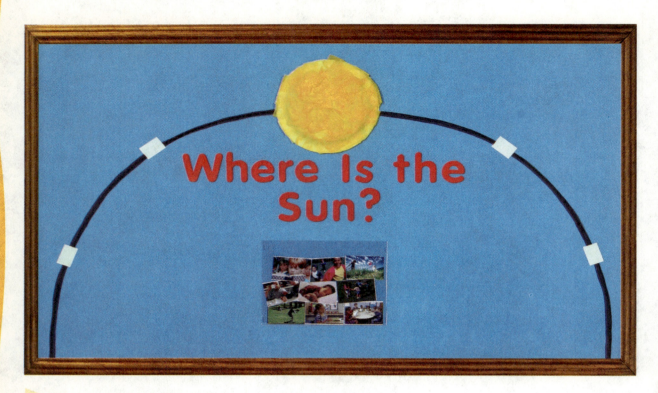

164 Solar System

See page 123 for materials list and directions.

169 Weather

See page 126 for materials list and directions.

175 Character Education

See page 129 for materials list and directions.

180 Communities

See page 132 for materials list and directions.

185 Economics

See page 135 for materials list and directions.

191 Government

See page 138 for materials list and directions.

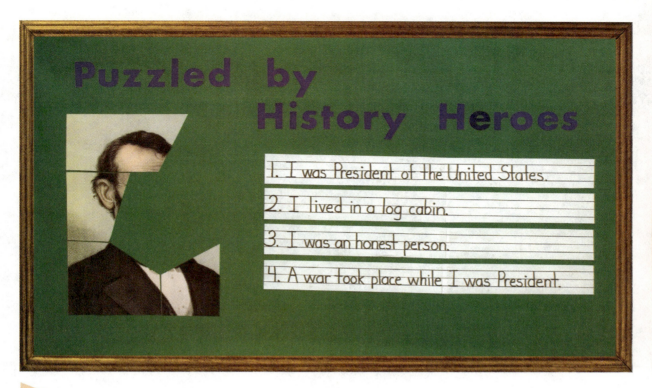

197 Heroes

See page 141 for materials list and directions.

202 Landforms and Water Bodies

See page 144 for materials list and directions.

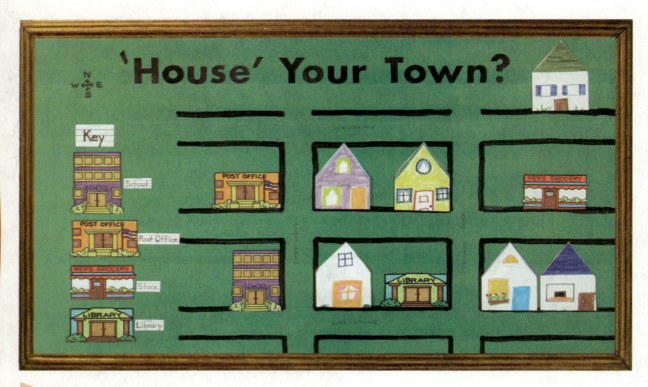

208 Map Skills

See page 147 for materials list and directions.

214 National Symbols

See page 150 for materials list and directions.

Alphabet

1 ▶ Fishin' for Definitions ✂✂✂

Language Arts Standard ▶ Uses alphabetical order to locate information

Materials

- fish pattern on page 153
- worm pattern on page 153
- blue craft paper
- border
- yarn
- pipe cleaners
- hole punch
- dictionary
- file folder
- scissors
- stapler
- crayons or markers

Teacher Preparation

▶ Cover a bulletin board with blue craft paper to look like water.

▶ Add a border and the title "Fishin' for Definitions."

▶ Cut the pipe cleaners in half and shape them into hooks. Tie the straight end of the hooks to a piece of yarn that resembles a fishing line.

▶ Staple each fishing line and hook from the top of the bulletin board to look as though the hooks are in the water. Vary the length of each fishing line and have the hook face out.

▶ Duplicate several fish (p. 153) and an equal number of copies of the worm (p. 153).

▶ Color, cut out, and laminate the patterns.

▶ Write a vocabulary word on each worm. Staple a worm on each of the hooks.

(page 13)

Fishin' for Definitions

▶ Write the definitions of the vocabulary words on the fish. Then punch a hole by the mouth of the fish.

▶ Staple the sides of the file folder together to form a pocket. Then staple the pocket near a corner of the bulletin board. Place the fish in the pocket when not in use.

▶ Place a dictionary near the bulletin board.

Student Directions

▶ Read the vocabulary words on the worms.

▶ Use the dictionary to find the definition of the words.

▶ Match the definitions and the words by hanging each fish on the correct hook.

Additional Language Arts Bulletin Board Ideas

2 ▶ Get Hooked on the ABCs ✂

Language Arts Standard ▶ **Recognizes uppercase and lowercase letters**

- Prepare a bulletin board with the desired color of craft paper. Add a border and the title "Get Hooked on the ABCs."
- Staple 26 alphabet cards of uppercase letters on the bulletin board at student's eye level.
- Cut pipe cleaners in half and shape them into hooks. Tape a hook on each alphabet card on the bulletin board so that the hook faces out.
- Duplicate, color, and cut out 26 fish (p. 153). If desired, have students help color and cut out the fish.
- Write a lowercase letter on each fish.
- Punch a hole in each fish's mouth.
- Invite students to match the lowercase letter on each fish to the correct partner letter on the bulletin board by hooking the fish to the card.

3 ▶ Putting Words in 'Alpha-bait-ical' Order ✂✂

Language Arts Standard ▶ **Knows the order of the alphabet**

- Prepare a bulletin board with blue craft paper, a border, and the title "Putting Words in 'Alpha-bait-ical' Order."
- Enlarge the girl fishing (p. 154). Color the picture. Staple it to the bulletin board.
- Duplicate several fish (p. 153). Color and cut them out.
- Write three words on each fish that can be alphabetized by the first two letters. Use words such as *need, nest,* and *neck*.
- Staple the fish on the water in a pleasing arrangement.
- Have students write each group of words on a sheet of paper in alphabetical order.

Content-Related Bulletin Board Ideas

4 ▶ The One That Got Away

Math Standard ▶ Measures length using standard units

▶ Prepare a bulletin board with blue craft paper. Add a border and the title "The One That Got Away."
▶ Enlarge the fish (page 153) to a specific length using inches or centimeters. Continue to enlarge the pattern to make several fish of different lengths.
▶ Color each fish a different color, cut them out, and staple them on the bulletin board.
▶ Provide students with paper, pencil, and a measuring tool such as a ruler, yardstick, or measuring tape. Invite them to measure each fish and write a sentence describing each fish, such as *The blue fish is six inches long*.

5 ▶ Let's Make It "Of-fish-al"!

Social Studies Standard ▶ Understands the process of voting in elections

▶ Prepare a bulletin board with the desired color of craft paper, a border, and the title "Let's Make It 'Of-fish-al'!" Draw a line down the middle.
▶ Lead a discussion with students about the voting process during a local, state, or national election.
▶ Select a topic or issue that interests the students and is one that they can vote on.
▶ Write the available choices on sentence strips. Then staple the sentence strips on each side of the bulletin board.
▶ Provide each student with a fish (p. 153) to be used as a ballot. Have them color and cut out their fish.
▶ Encourage students to think about the topic or issue and to decide how they will vote. Help them staple their fish on the bulletin board to indicate their vote.
▶ Count the "ballots" to determine which side has a majority.

Classroom Management

6 ▶ We're Catching On to Good Behavior

▶ Prepare a bulletin board with craft paper, a border, and the title "We're Catching On to Good Behavior."
▶ Provide each student with a copy of the girl fishing (p. 154).
▶ Have students draw a self-portrait the size of the girl's head on a sheet of paper. Then have them cut it out and glue it on the picture to look as though they are the one who is fishing. Invite them to color the picture and to write their name on the side of the boat.
▶ Duplicate the fish (p. 153) for each student. Have them color and cut it out.
▶ Have students glue their fish on their picture when they have mastered the targeted behavior.

Genres

7 ▸ Cool Flavors of Books ✂✂✂

Language Arts Standard ▸ Distinguishes among different types of books

Materials

- ice-cream label patterns on page 155
- cone pattern on page 156
- scoop of ice-cream pattern on page 156
- craft paper in ice-cream colors
- border
- 6 clean, 1-gallon ice-cream containers
- construction paper that matches the craft paper
- brown construction paper
- scissors
- glue
- crayons or markers
- pencils
- stapler

Teacher Preparation

▸ Prepare a bulletin board with six colors of craft paper. Form radial-shaped sections.

▸ Add a border and the title "Cool Flavors of Books."

▸ Duplicate the ice-cream labels (p. 155) and color them. Cut them out.

▸ Glue the labels on the ice-cream containers.

▸ Staple an ice-cream container in each section of the bulletin board.

▸ Make several templates of the cone (p. 156) and of the scoop of ice cream (p. 156).

Student Directions

▸ Trace a cone on brown construction paper. Cut it out.

▸ Decide what kind of book you read and in what section of the bulletin board it belongs. Trace a scoop of ice cream on a matching color of construction paper. Cut it out.

▸ Write the name of the book and the author on the scoop of ice cream.

▸ Glue the scoop of ice cream on the cone.

▸ Staple the cone to the correct section of the bulletin board.

(page 13)

Additional Language Arts Bulletin Board Ideas

8 ▶ Sweet Treat Books ✂

Language Arts Standard ▶ Tells fiction from nonfiction

▸ Prepare a bulletin board with two colors of craft paper. Cut the paper on the diagonal from the bottom left-hand corner to the top right-hand corner.

▸ Add a border and the title "Sweet Treat Books."

▸ Write and cut out the words *Real* and *Make-believe*. Staple the words to different corners of the bulletin board.

▸ Trace a cone (p. 156) on brown paper for each student. Cut out the cones.

▸ Display a shelf of fiction and nonfiction books. Have each student select one book from the shelf.

▸ Lead students in a discussion of ways to tell make-believe, or fiction, books from real, or nonfiction, books. Invite students to tell what kind of book they selected from the shelf.

▸ Have each student create a cover for a fiction or nonfiction book and color it. Then have students tell on which side of the bulletin board their cover belongs.

▸ Staple each cover on the bulletin board with a cone underneath.

9 ▶ Scoop Up a Good Book ✂✂

Language Arts Standard ▶ Recognizes the distinguishing features of familiar genres

▸ Prepare a bulletin board with the desired color of craft paper, a border, and the title "Scoop Up a Good Book."

▸ Enlarge the scoop (p. 218) and trace it on gray craft paper. Cut out the scoop and staple it to the center of the bulletin board.

▸ Make several templates of the cone (p. 156) and the scoop of ice cream (p. 156).

▸ Invite students to trace a cone on brown paper and a scoop of ice cream on a bright color of paper.

▸ Have them cut out the cones and scoops of ice cream and glue them together.

▸ Have students write the name of a book they read on the scoop of ice cream and the genre of the book on the cone.

▸ Allow students time to share a summary of their book and its genre.

▸ Staple the completed ice-cream cones to the bulletin board.

Content-Related Bulletin Board Ideas

10 ▶ We All Scream for Ice Cream!

Math Standard ▶ Constructs picture graphs

- ▶ Prepare a bulletin board with the desired color of craft paper, a border, and the title "We All Scream for Ice Cream!"
- ▶ Draw the outline for a picture graph that has four rows. Label the rows with these categories: *Vanilla*, *Chocolate*, *Strawberry*, and *Mint Chocolate Chip*.
- ▶ Write the title *Favorite Flavors of Ice Cream* above the graph.
- ▶ Make several templates of the cone (p. 156) and the scoop of ice cream (p. 156).
- ▶ Invite students to trace the cone on brown paper and the ice cream on a color of paper that matches their favorite flavor on the graph: white for vanilla, tan for chocolate, pink for strawberry, or light green for mint chocolate chip.
- ▶ Have students cut out the cone and ice cream and glue them together.
- ▶ Help students tape their ice-cream cones to the bulletin board in the appropriate category to form a picture graph.
- ▶ Ask students questions about the data.

11 ▶ Cooling Off on a Hot Day!

Science Standard ▶ Identifies that heat causes change

- ▶ Prepare a bulletin board with the desired color of craft paper, a border, and the title "Cooling Off on a Hot Day!"
- ▶ Enlarge the girl (p. 157). Color the figure and cut it out.
- ▶ Staple the figure to the bulletin board.
- ▶ Make several templates of the cone (p. 156) and the scoop of ice cream (p. 156).
- ▶ Have students trace the cone on brown paper and the ice cream on white paper.
- ▶ Tell students to color the ice cream with colored chalk.
- ▶ Have students place the ice cream in a self-sealing bag with a piece of ice on top of the bag.
- ▶ Lay the bags in a sunny place so that students can observe the changes, in both the ice and the chalk-colored scoop of ice cream.
- ▶ Discuss the changes to the ice and the ice cream.
- ▶ Have students remove their ice cream from the bag and glue it on their cone.
- ▶ Staple the ice-cream cones on the bulletin board in a pleasing arrangement.

Grammar

12 The Circus Is in Town ✂✂✂

Language Arts Standard ▶ **Composes elaborated sentences in writing**

Materials

lion pattern on page 168, seal pattern on page 158, horse pattern on page 158, elephant pattern on page 158, circle pattern on page 202, engine pattern on page 159, craft paper, border, clean styrofoam meat trays, rulers, hole punch, white and black construction paper, yarn, scissors, stapler, glue, pencils, crayons or markers, tape

Teacher Preparation

▶ Prepare a bulletin board with the desired color of craft paper, a border, and the title "The Circus Is in Town."

▶ Make several templates of the lion (p. 168), seal (p. 158), horse (p. 158), elephant (p. 158), and circle (p. 202). Duplicate the engine (p. 159) on white construction paper. Color and cut it out.

▶ Explain alliteration to the students. Review adjectives.

▶ Invite students to read their alliterative sentences and identify each adjective. Staple their cars to the bulletin board to form a circus train.

Student Directions

▶ Mark one-inch intervals along the top and bottom of a meat tray. Align the marks vertically. Punch a hole at each mark.

▶ Trace or draw a circus animal on white construction paper.

The Circus Is in Town

(page 14)

▶ Color and cut out the animal. Glue it on a meat tray.

▶ Write an alliterative sentence about the animal, using adjectives to describe how the animal looks or moves or what it does in the circus. Cut out a speech bubble from construction paper and write the alliterative sentence in the bubble. Glue it beside the animal on the meat tray.

▶ Cut a long piece of yarn. Tape one end to the back of the tray. Push the loose end through the nearest hole and pull it to the front of the tray. Push the yarn through the hole directly opposite to make a bar. Weave the yarn through all the holes to complete the bars on the train car. Tape the loose end of the yarn to the back of the tray.

▶ Trace two circles for wheels on black construction paper and cut them out. Glue them to the train car.

Additional Language Arts Bulletin Board Ideas

13 ► Big Sentences Under the Big Top ✂

Language Arts Standard ► Gains increasing control of grammar when speaking, such as complete sentences

- ▶ Prepare a bulletin board with the desired color of craft paper.
- ▶ For a border, accordion pleat long pieces of craft paper and staple them around the top and sides of the bulletin board to look like the folds of a circus tent.
- ▶ Add the title "Big Sentences Under the Big Top."
- ▶ Trace several lions (p. 168), dogs (p. 165), seals (p. 158), horses (p. 158), and elephants (p. 158) on white paper. Cut out the animals.
- ▶ Give each student a paper plate.
- ▶ Tell students that circuses used to perform in large tents called big tops.
- ▶ Invite students to choose the cutout of an animal that they would like to see at the circus. Have them color it and glue it to the center of the paper plate.
- ▶ Ask students to dictate a sentence telling why they want to see the animal and record their response on the outside ring of the paper plate.
- ▶ Invite each student to read his or her sentence before you staple it to the bulletin board.

14 ► "An-noun-cing" the Circus Fun ✂✂

Language Arts Standard ► Uses nouns and verbs in sentences

- ▶ Prepare a bulletin board with the desired color of craft paper, a border, and the title "'An-noun-cing' the Circus Fun."
- ▶ Trace a lion (p. 168), seal (p. 158), horse (p. 158), elephant (p. 158), and dog (p. 165) on white paper. Color and cut them out.
- ▶ Put one side of sticky hook and loop fastener tape on each animal.
- ▶ Enlarge the announcer (p. 158). Trace the announcer on white craft paper. Color and cut out the announcer.
- ▶ Staple the announcer to the center of the bulletin board.
- ▶ Write simple fill-in-the-blank sentences on sentence strips that describe actions the animals do, leaving out the nouns. Sentences might include *The [noun] has a ball* or *The [noun] jumps.*
- ▶ Leave a space for each noun that is wide enough so that students can use the paper animals to complete the sentences.
- ▶ Attach the other side of the sticky hook and loop fastener tape in the space on the sentence strip where the noun goes.
- ▶ Staple the sentence strips to the bulletin board.
- ▶ Staple the sides of a folder to use as a storage place for the animal cutouts. Staple the folder to one corner of the bulletin board.
- ▶ Put the animal cutouts in the folder. Invite students to attach the correct animals to the sentences as they read them.

Content-Related Bulletin Board Ideas

15 Balls of Fun

Math Standard ▶ Uses numbers to describe how many are in a set

▶ Prepare a bulletin board with the desired color of craft paper, a border, and the title "Balls of Fun." Duplicate 20 seals (p. 158) on gray paper and cut them out.
▶ Write a number from 1 to 20 on each seal.
▶ Cut out circles (p. 202) from different colors of paper to make balls.
▶ Staple the balls in stacks to show sets containing as many as 20 balls.
▶ Make pockets by cutting sentence strips in four-inch lengths and folding them lengthwise. Staple the pockets under the balls.
▶ Invite students to count the balls and place the seal with the correct number in the pocket underneath the stack.

16 Ticket Time

Social Studies Standard ▶ Explains how work provides income to purchase goods and services

▶ Prepare a bulletin board with the desired color of craft paper, a border, and the title "Ticket Time."
▶ Enlarge the announcer (p. 158) and trace the figure on white craft paper. Color and cut out the announcer.
▶ Draw a ticket shape and write *$15.00* on it.
▶ Staple the announcer to one side of the bulletin board and staple the ticket to the announcer's hand.
▶ Make a copy of the chart below and staple it to the opposite side of the bulletin board.
▶ Provide each student with a copy of the chart.
▶ Tell students to choose jobs they can do and think of the number of times they would have to do each job to save enough money to buy a $15.00 circus ticket. Explain they can save more than $15.00.
▶ Have students record the information on their own chart.
▶ Invite students to draw a picture of themselves doing one of the jobs.
▶ Staple students' charts and pictures to the bulletin board.

Jobs

Job	Pay
Wash dishes	$1.00
Sweep kitchen	$0.50
Take out trash	$0.25
Walk dog	$0.50
Weed garden	$1.00
Fold clothes	$0.75

Parts of a Book

17 Terrific Titles, Awesome Authors, and Illustrious Illustrators ✄✄

Language Arts Standard ▶ **Understands simple literary terms such as title, author, and illustrator**

Materials

- book cover pattern on page 160
- craft paper
- border
- white construction paper
- storybooks
- scissors
- stapler
- pencils
- crayons or markers

Teacher Preparation

▶ Prepare a bulletin board with the desired color of craft paper, a border, and the title "Terrific Titles, Awesome Authors, and Illustrious Illustrators."

▶ Duplicate a book cover (p. 160) on construction paper for each student.

▶ Provide students with a selection of storybooks.

▶ When students have completed their book covers, staple them on the bulletin board.

Student Directions

▶ Read a book.

▶ Color and cut out the book cover pattern.

▶ Write the title, author, and illustrator of your book on the cover.

▶ Read the title, author, and illustrator aloud to the class as your book cover is stapled to the bulletin board.

(page 14)

   Bulletin Boards, SV 1-4190-1884-1

Additional Language Arts Bulletin Board Ideas

18 ▶ You, Too, Can Be an Author or Illustrator ✂

Language Arts Standard ▶ Distinguishes between the roles of the author and the illustrator

▸ Prepare a bulletin board with the desired color of craft paper. Add a border and the title "You, Too, Can Be an Illustrator."
▸ Read a variety of books to students.
▸ Explain to them that the author writes the story and the illustrator draws the pictures. Often one person is the author of a book and a different person is the illustrator. However, authors such as Jan Brett and Eric Carle write *and* illustrate their own stories.
▸ Invite students to become authors and illustrators. Ask them to write or dictate a sentence telling about their favorite activity such as jumping rope or playing ball. Then have them illustrate their sentence.
▸ Staple students' sentences and illustrations on the bulletin board.

19 ▶ Know Where to Look in a Book ✂✂✂

Language Arts Standard ▶ Uses the table of contents to locate information

▸ Prepare a bulletin board with the desired color of craft paper, a border, and the title "Know Where to Look in a Book."
▸ Enlarge the open book (p. 161) to a desired size.
▸ Write the table of contents below on the pages of the book.
▸ Staple the book in the middle of the bulletin board.
▸ Write the topics from the table of contents on sentence strips. Cut the strips apart so that each topic is on a separate strip. Staple the topics around the open book.
▸ Write questions about the topics on index cards.
▸ Have students take turns picking a card and answering the question using the information on the table of contents.
▸ Invite students to write the topics and the page numbers that answer the questions on a separate sheet of paper.
▸ Store the index cards in a file folder that is stapled to the bulletin board.

Table of Contents

Content-Related Bulletin Board Ideas

20 ▶ The Total Points of the Title

Math Standard ▶ **Solves multiplication problems with one-digit multiplier**

- ▶ Prepare a bulletin board with the desired color of craft paper, a border, and the title "The Total Points of the Title."
- ▶ Write the following codes on sentence strips: *Vowels = 5 points, Consonants = 4 points*. Staple the sentence strips on the bulletin board.
- ▶ Duplicate the book cover pattern (p. 160) and white-out the author and illustrator.
- ▶ Enlarge several copies of the book cover on light colored paper. Cut out the book covers.
- ▶ Select familiar stories that have several words in the title, such as *And to Think That I Saw It on Mulberry Street*.
- ▶ Write a title on each book cover and staple each one on the bulletin board.
- ▶ Challenge students to count the vowels in the title and multiply by 5 to get a total.
- ▶ Then have them count the consonants and multiply by 4 to get a total.
- ▶ Have students add the vowels total and the consonants total to find the total point value of each title.

21 ▶ Reading Up on Skeletons

Science Standard ▶ **Identifies characteristics of living organisms**

- ▶ Prepare a bulletin board with the desired color of craft paper, a border, and the title "Reading Up on Skeletons."
- ▶ Provide reference books that show a variety of animal skeletons.
- ▶ Lead a discussion with students about the size, shape, and function of bones and how bones give animals their shape.
- ▶ Duplicate the open book pattern (p. 161) for each student. Have them cut out the book.
- ▶ Have students draw a picture of a skeleton of their favorite animal on one page of their book. Then have them write the name of the animal on the other page.
- ▶ Staple their books on the bulletin board.

Phonics

22 ▶ On the Phone with Phonics ✂

Language Arts Standard ▶ Recognizes beginning consonants

Materials

- girl talking on phone pattern on page 162
- white craft paper
- border
- magazines
- small index cards
- overhead projector
- glue
- scissors
- stapler
- self-stick adhesive tape
- pencils
- crayons or markers

Teacher Preparation

▶ Prepare a bulletin board with craft paper, a border, and the title "On the Phone with Phonics."

▶ Enlarge the girl pattern (p. 162) to the desired size. Color and cut out the pattern.

▶ Staple the girl on the left side of the bulletin board.

▶ Draw a large speech bubble near the girl's mouth.

▶ Cut out pictures from a magazine of items whose names begin with targeted consonant sounds.

▶ Glue the pictures in a pleasing arrangement in the speech bubble.

▶ Write the beginning consonant on a separate index card for each picture name.

▶ Place self-stick adhesive tape on the back of each index card.

Student Directions

▶ Say the name of each picture in the speech bubble.

▶ Attach the beginning sounds on the index cards to the correct pictures.

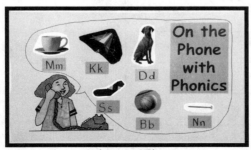

(page 15)

Bulletin Boards, SV 1-4190-1884-1

Additional Language Arts Bulletin Board Ideas

23 ▶ The Phone "Consonant-ly" Rings ✂✂

Language Arts Standard ▶ Recognizes letter-sound correspondences including consonant blends

- ▶ Prepare a bulletin board with the desired color of craft paper. Add a border and the title "The Phone 'Consonant-ly' Rings."
- ▶ Duplicate and cut out several telephone receivers and bases (p. 163). Staple the bases on the bulletin board. Leave space for the receivers.
- ▶ Select several beginning or final consonant blends as target sounds. Cut out pictures from magazines of objects whose names contain examples of the target sounds. Attach a picture to each base with self-stick adhesive tape.
- ▶ Use a washable marker to write the targeted blends for the pictures on the receivers. Attach self-stick adhesive tape on the back of the receivers.
- ▶ Invite students to match the blends with the pictures by placing the receivers on the correct telephone bases.

24 ▶ Text Message a Digraph Clue ✂✂✂

Language Arts Standard ▶ Recognizes letter-sound correspondences including consonant digraphs

- ▶ Prepare a bulletin board with the desired color of craft paper, a border, and the title "Text Message a Digraph Clue." Draw a line to divide the bulletin board in half.
- ▶ Write the two questions and the directions from the chart below on separate sentence strips. Staple the sentence strips in columns according to the chart.
- ▶ Duplicate the cell phone (p. 163) twice. Color and cut out the phones. Staple a cell phone in each column next to each set of directions.
- ▶ Write *knock* on the screen of the cell phone in the left column and *fish* on the screen of the cell phone in the right column.
- ▶ Invite students to read the questions and the clues. Have them use a washable marker and write each new word on the lines.

What can you do with a bell?	What do you do with a ball?
Change **kn** to **s**. _____	Change **f** to **w**. _____
Change **ck** to **ng**. _____	Change **i** to **a**. _____
Change **s** to **wr**. _____	Change **sh** to **tch**. _____
Change **o** to **i**. _____	Change **w** to **p**. _____
Change **wr** to **r**. _____	Change **a** to **i**. _____

Content-Related Bulletin Board Ideas

25 ▸ Dialing for Dollars

Math Standard ▸ Determines the value of a collection of coins

- Prepare a bulletin board with the desired color of craft paper, a border, and the title "Dialing for Dollars."
- Duplicate, color, and cut out several telephone receivers and bases (p. 163). Staple the telephones in a pleasing arrangement on the bulletin board.
- Duplicate a supply of money patterns (p. 192) that includes coins and dollars. Color and cut them out. Stick self-adhesive tape on the back of the dollars.
- Glue a different combination of coins on each base. Have most of the coin combinations total one dollar and have the other combinations total less than one dollar.
- Stick self-adhesive tape on the back of the dollar patterns.
- Invite students to find the total value of the coins on each base. Then have them attach the dollar on the receivers of the bases that total one dollar.

26 ▸ Let's Talk About Plants

Science Standard ▸ Identifies external characteristics of plants

- Prepare a bulletin board with the desired color of craft paper, a border, and the title "Let's Talk About Plants."
- Enlarge the girl (p. 162). Color and cut out the figure. Staple it in the center of the bulletin board.
- Lead a discussion with students about the parts of a plant. Invite each student to draw and label a picture showing the parts of a plant.
- Staple students' pictures on the bulletin board.

27 ▸ Telephone or Computer

Social Studies Standard ▸ Describes how technology has changed communication

- Prepare a bulletin board with the desired color of craft paper, a border, and the title "Telephone or Computer."
- Enlarge the telephone (p. 163) and the computer (p. 164) to the desired size. Color and cut them out. Then staple them side by side on the bulletin board.
- Cut a spiral circle and attach the ends to the receiver and the base of the telephone to resemble the cord.
- Cut several sentence strips in half. Write fictitious telephone numbers on half of them. Write fictitious web sites and e-mail addresses on the other half.
- Stick self-adhesive tape on the back of the sentence strips.
- Invite students to determine which information is needed for the telephone and which is needed for the computer. Have students place the sentence strips by the correct picture.

Punctuation

28 ▸ Doggone Good Sentences ✄✄

Language Arts Standard ▸ Uses correct ending punctuation

Materials

- animal face patterns on page 165
- bone pattern on page 191
- craft paper
- border
- brown lunch sacks
- scissors
- brown, tan, white, and black construction paper
- stapler
- glue
- pencils
- crayons or markers

Teacher Preparation

▸ Prepare a bulletin board with the desired color of craft paper, a border, and the title "Doggone Good Sentences."

▸ Make several templates of the animal face patterns (p. 165).

▸ Duplicate and cut out bones (p. 191) from tan construction paper. Make enough bones to place them end to end to form lines that divide the bulletin board into four equal sections. Staple the bones in an X or + position on the bulletin board.

▸ Label two opposite sections with a period (.). Label the other two with a question mark (?) and an exclamation point (!).

▸ Review with students the four kinds of sentences: statement, question, exclamation, and command.

▸ Invite students to share their sentence. Have them tell what kind of sentence they wrote and help them staple it to the correct part of the bulletin board.

Student Directions

▸ Trace and cut out two ears, two eyes, a tongue, and a nose from the desired colors of construction paper.

▸ Glue them on a lunch sack to make a dog puppet.

(page 15)

▸ Draw and cut out additional features if desired, such as whiskers, spots, or toys with which a dog might play.

▸ Imagine the dog puppet comes to life. What does it say? Write a statement, question, exclamation, or command that the dog says on the body of the dog.

Additional Language Arts Bulletin Board Ideas

29 ▶ I "Spot" a Sentence! ✂

Language Arts Standard ▶ Recognizes how readers use punctuation

▶ Prepare a bulletin board with the desired color of craft paper, a border, and the title "I 'Spot' a Sentence!" Enlarge the girl and dog (p. 166) and trace the figures on craft paper. Color the girl and the dog, adding spots to the dog. Cut out the figures and staple them to the bulletin board.

▶ Trace a dog (p. 165) on white paper for each student and then cut out all the dogs.

▶ Cut strips of brown craft paper for each student for leashes.

▶ Have students color their dog so it has spots.

▶ Invite students to dictate or write a sentence about a dog named Spot on their dogs.

▶ Point out the punctuation at the end of each sentence.

▶ Staple all the dogs and leashes to the girl's hand.

30 ▶ "Paws" for Commas ✂✂✂

Language Arts Standard ▶ Uses commas in a series

▶ Prepare a bulletin board with the desired color of craft paper and the title "'Paws' for Commas."

▶ Trace and cut out multiple copies of the paw print (p. 167) in any paper color to use as a border. Also make several templates of a reduced size paw print.

▶ Enlarge the girl and dog (p. 166) and trace them on white craft paper. Color both figures and cut them out.

▶ Cut around the leash to remove it from both figures.

▶ Staple the girl to one side of the bulletin board and the dog on the other side.

▶ Challenge students to think of three things a dog can do or places it can visit while running free. Have them each write a sentence on a sentence strip identifying the three activities or places.

▶ Tell students to trace and cut out two paw prints, write a comma on each paw print, and glue them to the sentence strip to show where commas belong in a series.

▶ Staple the sentences to the middle of the bulletin board.

Content-Related Bulletin Board Ideas

31 ► "Spotting" Fractions

Math Standard ► Names fractional parts of a set of objects

- ► Prepare a bulletin board with the desired color of craft paper, a border, and the title "'Spotting' Fractions."
- ► Staple an envelope to the bulletin board.
- ► Make several templates of the dog (p. 165).
- ► Invite students to trace a dog on white paper and color it. Have students use two colors of markers to draw spots on the dog's body to show fractional parts up to tenths.
- ► Tell students to write the different fractions on index cards for their own dog.
- ► Staple the dogs to the bulletin board. Put the index cards in the envelope.
- ► Challenge students to match the index cards to the correct dogs. Have students slide the cards between the dog's body and the tail.

32 ► Home, Sweet Home

Science Standard ► Compares living organisms and nonliving objects

- ► Prepare a bulletin board with the desired color of craft paper, a border, and the title "Home, Sweet Home."
- ► Enlarge the dog (p. 165) and doghouse (p. 167) and trace them on white craft paper. Color and cut them out. Staple the figures to the center of the bulletin board.
- ► Tell students that the dog is a living organism because it breathes, eats, and moves. Explain that the doghouse is not alive and is classified as an object.
- ► Then invite students to think of other animals and the animal homes they live in. Tell students to draw and color pictures of the animals and their homes.
- ► Ask students to share their pictures and explain which is a living organism and which is an object.
- ► Staple students' pictures to the bulletin board.

Reading Comprehension

33 ▸ Here's the "Mane" Idea ✂✂

Language Arts Standard ▸ Makes and explains inferences from texts, such as determining important ideas

Materials

- lion face patterns on page 168
- green craft paper
- border
- paper plates
- yellow and white construction paper
- scissors
- stapler
- glue
- pencils
- crayons or markers
- nonfiction article

Teacher Preparation

▸ Prepare a bulletin board with green craft paper, a border, and the title "Here's the 'Mane' Idea."

▸ Provide a nonfiction article for students to read.

▸ Duplicate the eyes, ears, nose, and mouth (p. 168) on white construction paper for each student.

▸ Cut the yellow paper into 4" x 2" strips. Give each student 10 strips.

▸ Staple students' completed lions to the bulletin board.

Student Directions

▸ Color the front of a paper plate yellow.

▸ Color and cut out the patterns. Glue them on the paper plate.

▸ Read the nonfiction article. Think about the main idea. Look for details that tell about the main idea.

▸ Write the main idea on the face of the lion.

(page 16)

▸ Get 10 strips of yellow construction paper. Write four or more details about the main idea on different strips.

▸ Glue all the strips around the lion's face to make the mane.

Additional Language Arts Bulletin Board Ideas

34 ▶ Tell a Tale ✂

Language Arts Standard ▶ Retells the important events in a story

- ▶ Prepare a bulletin board with the desired color of craft paper, a border, and the title "Tell a Tale."
- ▶ Trace and cut out a set of lion face patterns (p. 168) from white paper for each student. Color them.
- ▶ Cut yellow paper into 4" x 2" strips for the mane.
- ▶ Enlarge and duplicate the four picture cards (p. 169). Color, cut out, and laminate the cards. Then punch a large hole at the top of each card.
- ▶ Attach four self-stick hooks to the bulletin board at intervals at students' eye level.
- ▶ Share the story of *The Lion and the Mouse*, hanging the cards on the hooks in order as you tell it.
- ▶ Invite students to make a paper plate lion as described in "Here's the 'Mane' Idea" on page 51.
- ▶ Staple the paper plate lions in a pleasing arrangement on the bulletin board.
- ▶ Allow students to use the picture cards to retell the story as they hang the cards on the hooks in order.

35 ▶ Hunting for the Facts ✂✂✂

Language Arts Standard ▶ Distinguishes fact from opinion

- ▶ Prepare a bulletin board with yellow craft paper, a border, and the title "Hunting for the Facts."
- ▶ Cut two additional pieces of yellow craft paper the length of the bulletin board. Fringe them to resemble savanna grasses and staple them to the bulletin board. Write *Fact* on one length and *Opinion* on the other.
- ▶ Next make several templates of the lion (p. 168).
- ▶ Have students trace a lion on yellow paper and cut it out.
- ▶ Invite them to write a sentence on the lion stating a fact or an opinion about a topic related to an area of study.
- ▶ Have students share their sentences, allowing classmates to identify the sentences as facts or opinions.
- ▶ Help students staple their lions in the correct corresponding savanna grass to look as if they are hiding.

Content-Related Bulletin Board Ideas

36 ► Family Pride

Math Standard ► **Identifies patterns in related addition and subtraction sentences**

- ► Prepare a bulletin board with yellow craft paper. Add a border and the title "Family Pride."
- ► Cut out at least five irregular shapes from blue craft paper to represent water holes. Staple them in different places on the bulletin board.
- ► Write the three numbers belonging to a fact family on each water hole.
- ► Make several templates of the lion (p. 168).
- ► Have students trace and cut out a lion from yellow paper and write a math fact using a set of numbers they have chosen from a water hole.
- ► Next tell students that a family of lions is called a pride and that related numbers are known as fact families.
- ► Invite students to match the math fact on their lion with the fact family on the water hole. Help them staple the math fact to the correct water hole.
- ► When the bulletin board is complete, challenge students to find any pride that is missing one related number sentence.

37 ► Asking the King of the Jungle

Science Standard ► **Asks questions about organisms, objects, and events**

- ► Prepare a bulletin board with green craft paper. Cut strips of green and brown crepe streamers and staple them along the top of the bulletin board so they hang down to look like jungle vines. Add a border and the title "Asking the King of the Jungle."
- ► Enlarge the lion (p. 168). Trace the figure on craft paper. Color and cut out the lion. Staple it to one side of the bulletin board.
- ► Make a king's crown by twisting foil and gluing sequins to the foil. Attach it to the lion's head.
- ► Cut out a large scroll shape from white craft paper. Write a science question that might interest students at the top of the scroll. Invite students to write other science questions on the scroll that they would like to have answered.
- ► Challenge students to find the answers to the questions through research using computers or books. Have students write the answers on index cards. Staple the index cards next to the questions on the bulletin board.

Research

38 ▶ **Spiders Are Good Researchers . . . They Make Webs!** ✂✂✂

Language Arts Standard ▶ **Organizes information in systematic ways**

Materials

- spider pattern on page 170
- circle pattern on page 202
- craft paper
- border
- white construction paper
- white yarn
- scissors
- crayons or markers
- stapler

Teacher Preparation

▶ Prepare a bulletin board with the desired color of craft paper and a border.

▶ Use white yarn to make a large orb web that covers the bulletin board.

▶ Enlarge the spider (p. 170) and trace it on white construction paper. Color the figure and cut it out. Staple the spider to one side of the bulletin board.

▶ Add the title "Spiders Are Good Researchers . . . They Make Webs!"

▶ Write a main idea topic on white paper and staple it to the center of the web.

▶ Duplicate a circle (p. 202) for each student on white construction paper.

▶ Discuss the use of a web when organizing ideas for research.

Student Directions

▶ Look at the main idea written on the web. Think about details that tell about the main idea.

▶ Cut out a circle.

▶ Write a detail on the circle. Use a complete sentence.

▶ Staple the detail to the web.

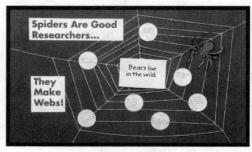

(page 16)

Additional Language Arts Bulletin Board Ideas

39 "Spider-ific" Facts ✂

Language Arts Standard ▶ Uses pictures, print, and people to gather information and answer questions

- ▶ Prepare a bulletin board with the desired color of craft paper.
- ▶ Use white chalk to draw a large web on the entire bulletin board. Add a border and the title "Spider-ific Facts."
- ▶ Next use a white crayon to trace a spider body (p. 171) on black paper for each student. Cut out the spiders.
- ▶ Cut black paper lengthwise into half-inch strips to make legs. Each student will need eight strips.
- ▶ Provide resources about spiders that you read aloud or that students review on their own.
- ▶ Invite each student to write or dictate a fact about spiders, writing the sentence on the spider with white chalk or crayon.
- ▶ Tell students to accordion pleat four paper strips to make legs and glue them on the underside of the largest part of the spider's body.
- ▶ Help students read their sentence before stapling the spiders to the bulletin board.

40 We Spin Good Questions ✂✂

Language Arts Standard ▶ Identifies relevant questions for study

- ▶ Prepare a bulletin board with light blue craft paper and a border. Add the title "We Spin Good Questions."
- ▶ Make trees to fill the bulletin board by crumpling brown craft paper for the trunks and green craft paper for the treetops. Staple them to the bulletin board.
- ▶ Next duplicate a spider (p. 170) and a fly (p. 170) for each student. Then have students color the spider and the fly.
- ▶ Have students cut out the center of a paper plate and punch holes around the remaining perimeter. Tell students to weave white yarn through the holes from one side to the other to make a spider's web.
- ▶ Ask students to write a question about spiders on the spider's body.
- ▶ Then have students attach their spider to the web.
- ▶ Invite students to share their questions before stapling the webs on the trees.
- ▶ During free time, challenge students to research the questions and record the answers on the flies, which they will attach to the appropriate webs.

Content-Related Bulletin Board Ideas

41   We "Spy-der" Legs!

Math Standard ▶ **Generates a table of paired numbers based on real-life situations**

- Prepare a bulletin board with the desired color of craft paper, a border, and the title "We 'Spy-der' Legs!"
- Use chalk to draw four large webs on the bulletin board so that there is one web in each corner. Number them from 1 to 4.
- Make several templates of the spider body (p. 171).
- Invite students to trace the body on black, brown, green, or gray paper using a white crayon. Tell them to cut the body out.
- Have students cut eight strips from the same color of paper to make legs. Tell students to accordion pleat the legs and glue them to the underside of the largest part of the spider's body.
- Have students punch a hole in eight white circles and glue them to the spider to make compound eyes.
- Invite students to group the completed spiders by color and staple them to the webs.
- Tell students to number a sheet of paper from 1 to 4.
- Challenge them to make tables to show the correlation of spiders to legs on each web.

42   Spiders Are Everywhere!

Science Standard ▶ **Identifies the external characteristics of different kinds of animals that allow their needs to be met**

- Prepare a bulletin board with white craft paper and paint a nature scene that includes brown tree trunks, green treetops, green bushes, and gray rocks. Add a border and the title "Spiders Are Everywhere!"
- Make templates of the spider body (p. 171).
- Invite students to trace the body on black, brown, green, or gray paper using a white crayon. Tell them to cut the body out.
- Have students cut eight strips from the same color of paper to make legs. Tell students to accordion pleat the legs and glue them to the underside of the largest part of the spider's body.
- Have students punch a hole in eight white circles and glue them to the spider to make compound eyes.
- Discuss with students the different colors of spiders. Guide them to understand that spiders often live in places where they blend into their surroundings. For example, tell students that gray spiders usually live in rocks and green spiders often live in bushes and treetops.
- Challenge students to choose a place on the bulletin board where their spiders can live safely. Staple their spiders there.

Rhyming Words

43 ▸ The Cat's Hat Is Full of Rhymes ✂✂

Language Arts Standard ▸ **Produces rhyming words**

Materials

- hat pattern on page 172
- cat pattern on page 173
- blue craft paper
- border
- overhead projector
- white poster board
- washable marker

- permanent marker
- nail polish remover
- paper towels
- scissors
- stapler
- crayons or markers

Teacher Preparation

- ▸ Cover a bulletin board with blue craft paper.
- ▸ Enlarge the cat (p. 173) and the hat (p. 172) on the poster board.
- ▸ Color, cut out, and laminate the patterns.
- ▸ Staple the hat on the cat's head and place both in the middle of the bulletin board.
- ▸ Add a border and the title "The Cat's Hat Is Full of Rhymes."
- ▸ Use the permanent marker to write a target word family on each stripe on the hat. Leave the beginning sound blank such as ___ *at*.
- ▸ Change the word family by cleaning off the hat with nail polish remover when students are not in the classroom.

Student Directions

- ▸ Use the washable marker to write rhyming words on the cat's hat.
- ▸ Read your words to a friend.
- ▸ Dampen a paper towel with water and clean off the hat.

(page 17)

Additional Language Arts Bulletin Board Ideas

44 Serving Up Rhyming Words ✂

Language Standard ▶ Recognizes rhyming words

- ▶ Prepare a bulletin board with the desired color of craft paper. Add a border and the title "Serving Up Rhyming Words."
- ▶ Read *Green Eggs and Ham* to students. Discuss the words that rhyme in the story.
- ▶ Duplicate and cut out several plates of ham (p. 173) and eggs (p. 172). Color the ham and eggs green and laminate them.
- ▶ Cut out pictures from a magazine or draw pictures of objects whose names rhyme, such as a tree and a key.
- ▶ Glue one of the pictures on the ham and the other on the egg.
- ▶ Staple all of the plates of ham in a pleasing arrangement on the bulletin board.
- ▶ Place self-stick adhesive tape on the back of the eggs.
- ▶ Have students match the eggs with the hams whose picture names rhyme.

45 Dr. Seuss Is on the Loose ✂✂✂

Language Arts Standard ▶ Recognizes rhyming words

- ▶ Prepare a bulletin board with the desired color of craft paper, a border, and the title "Dr. Seuss Is on the Loose."
- ▶ Duplicate the hat (p. 172) for each student. Have students color and cut out their hats.
- ▶ Invite them to read their favorite Dr. Seuss book.
- ▶ Then have students write the title of their book on the brim of the hat.
- ▶ Challenge students to write a pair of rhyming words from their book on each stripe on the hat.
- ▶ Staple the hats in a pleasing arrangement on the bulletin board.

Content-Related Bulletin Board Ideas

46 ▶ Our Writing Is "Egg-ceptional"

Language Arts Standard ▶ Gains increasing control of aspects of penmanship

- ▶ Prepare a bulletin board with the desired color of craft paper. Add the title "Our Writing Is 'Egg-ceptional.'"
- ▶ Duplicate two or three eggs (p. 172) for each student. Have students color the yolks yellow and cut out each egg.
- ▶ Staple the eggs around the edge of the bulletin board for the border.
- ▶ Staple on the bulletin board an example of each student's work that shows good handwriting.

Math

47 ▶ Numbers Are More or Less "Purr-fect"

Math Standard ▶ Orders whole numbers using < and >

- ▶ Prepare a bulletin board with the desired color of craft paper. Add a border and the title "Numbers Are More or Less 'Purr-fect.'"
- ▶ Duplicate the cat (page 173) for each student. Have them color and cut out the cat.
- ▶ Instruct students to write a < sign or a > sign on the center section of each cat's bow tie.
- ▶ Give each student an index card on which two different numbers are written.
- ▶ Have students write their two numbers on the correct side of the greater than or less than sign on the bow tie.
- ▶ Staple students' completed cats on the bulletin board.

Social Studies

48 ▶ Hats Off to Good Citizens

Social Studies Standard ▶ Identifies historical figures who have exemplified good citizenship

- ▶ Prepare a bulletin board with the desired color of craft paper, a border, and the title "Hats Off to Good Citizens."
- ▶ Duplicate the hat (p. 172) for each student. Have students color and cut out their hat.
- ▶ Invite students to select a historic figure who exhibited good citizenship, such as Clara Barton, Nathan Hale, or Eleanor Roosevelt. Have students draw a picture of the person and write a sentence, telling what that person did that was an example of good citizenship.
- ▶ Staple students' completed work and their hats in a pleasing arrangement on the bulletin board.

Spelling

49 ▶ Take a Crack at Plurals ✂✂

Language Arts Standard ▶ **Writes with more proficient spelling of plurals**

Materials

- cracked egg pattern on page 174
- craft paper
- border
- green and white construction paper
- writing paper
- scissors
- stapler
- pencils
- crayons or markers

Teacher Preparation

- ▶ Prepare a bulletin board with the desired color of craft paper, a border, and the title "Take a Crack at Plurals."
- ▶ Cut the green construction paper in strips. Then fringe cut it to resemble grass. Staple two or three rows of grass so that the bulletin board will be evenly covered with the eggs.
- ▶ Duplicate several copies of the cracked egg (p. 174) on white construction paper. Enlarge and color if desired.
- ▶ Cut the eggs out, leaving them whole.
- ▶ Write a root word on the top half of each egg. Include words that have –s and –es plurals.
- ▶ Staple the eggs in the grass in a pleasing arrangement.
- ▶ When students have completed their lists, write the plurals of the root words on the bottom half of the eggs. Have students check their answers.
- ▶ Staple students' work on the bulletin board as part of the border.

Student Directions

- ▶ Read the root words on the bulletin board.
- ▶ Write the plural of each of the words on a sheet of paper.
- ▶ Check the bulletin board for the correct answers.

(page 17)

Additional Language Arts Bulletin Board Ideas

50 ▶ Building Our Families ✂

Language Arts Standard ▶ **Begins to spell some words using common phonograms**

▶ Prepare a bulletin board with the desired color of craft paper. Add a border and the title "Building Our Families."
▶ Cut small strips of brown paper and staple them on the bulletin board to resemble a nest. Make several nests.
▶ Duplicate a duck and wing (p. 175) for each nest. Color and cut them out.
▶ Fold back the legs so that the ducks can sit on the nest. Attach the wings to the bodies with brads.
▶ Write targeted phonograms such as *–at* or *–og* on the wings of the ducks.
▶ Staple a duck on each nest.
▶ Duplicate three or four eggs (p. 174) for each student. Have students cut out the eggs.
▶ Invite students to write words on their eggs that contain the targeted phonograms.
▶ Have students tell with which duck their egg goes. Help students staple their eggs in the correct nests.

51 ▶ "Waddle" We Do with Homonyms? ✂✂✂

Language Arts Standard ▶ **Writes with more proficient spelling of homonyms**

▶ Prepare a bulletin board with the desired color of craft paper, a border, and the title "'Waddle' We Do with Homonyms?"
▶ Cut green paper into strips. Then fringe the paper to resemble grass.
▶ Staple the grass across the bottom of the bulletin board.
▶ Duplicate several copies of the walking duck (p. 174). Color and cut them out.
▶ Write a pair of homonyms such as *meet, meat; tail, tale;* and *bear, bare* on each duck.
▶ Staple the ducks as though they are walking in a row through the grass.
▶ Invite students to read the homonyms aloud.
▶ Challenge students to write sentences using the homonyms and then to read them aloud.

Content-Related Bulletin Board Ideas

52 What an Odd Duck!

Math Standard ▶ Identifies numbers as odd or even

- ▶ Prepare a bulletin board with the desired color of craft paper, a border, and the title "What an Odd Duck!"
- ▶ Duplicate the egg several times (p. 174).
- ▶ Staple the eggs on the bulletin board in stacks. Make some stacks with an odd number of eggs and some with an even number.
- ▶ Cut sentence strips in six-inch lengths and fold them lengthwise to form pockets. Staple them below the stacks of eggs.
- ▶ Duplicate a duck and wing (p. 175) on yellow paper for each stack of eggs, and then count them out. Attach the wings to the bodies with brads.
- ▶ Write the words *odd* or *even* on each wing to match the stacks.
- ▶ Invite students to count the eggs to determine if the stack has an odd number of eggs or an even number. Challenge students to place a duck with the correct answer on its wing in each pocket.

53 Be "Eggs-tra" Sure About Your Measurements

Science Standard ▶ Measures objects using nonstandard units

- ▶ Prepare a bulletin board with the desired color of craft paper, a border, and the title "Be 'Eggs-tra' Sure About Your Measurements."
- ▶ Enlarge and reduce the egg (p. 174) so that there are a variety of sizes. Then cut them out and number the eggs. Staple the eggs to the bulletin board.
- ▶ Invite students to measure each egg using a nonstandard unit such as a paper clip. Then have them record the information on a sheet of paper.
- ▶ Staple students' papers on the bulletin board in a pleasing arrangement.

Classroom Management

54 We're Not Ducking Our Responsibility

- ▶ Prepare a bulletin board with the desired color of craft paper, a border, and the title "We're Not Ducking Our Responsibility."
- ▶ Duplicate the duck body (p. 175) for each student. Have them color and cut it out. Instruct students to write their name on the duck.
- ▶ Staple the ducks on the bulletin board in a pleasing arrangement.
- ▶ Lead a discussion with students about taking responsibility for turning in homework assignments.
- ▶ Have students tape a colored craft feather on their duck each day that they turn in their homework.
- ▶ You may wish to reward students with extra free time when they accumulate a designated number of feathers.

Vocabulary

55 Look How We "Fix" Words ✂✂

Language Arts Standard ▶ **Recognizes high-frequency words**

Materials

- carpenter pattern on page 176
- board pattern on page 176
- craft paper
- overhead projector
- border

- yellow construction paper
- scissors
- crayons or markers
- stapler
- white craft paper

Teacher Preparation

▶ Prepare a bulletin board with the desired color of craft paper, a border, and the title "Look How We 'Fix' Words."

▶ Enlarge the carpenter (p. 176) and trace the figure on white craft paper. Color and cut out the carpenter. Staple it to the bulletin board.

▶ Duplicate two boards (p. 176) on yellow construction paper for each student.

▶ Discuss prefixes and suffixes with students and provide examples.

▶ Staple students' completed boards to the bulletin board.

Student Directions

▶ Think of two words that have prefixes or suffixes. Write each word on a separate board.

▶ Cut the board between the root and its affix.

▶ Share your words and their meanings with the class.

(page 18)

Additional Language Arts Bulletin Board Ideas

56 ▷ Words to Build On ✂

Language Arts Standard ▶ Recognizes high-frequency words

- ▶ Prepare a bulletin board with the desired color of craft paper, a border, and the title "Words to Build On."
- ▶ Enlarge the bricklayer (p. 177). Trace the figure on white craft paper. Color and cut it out.
- ▶ Staple the bricklayer to one side of the bulletin board.
- ▶ Next cut rectangles out of red paper to make bricks.
- ▶ Write sight words that students are learning on the bricks.
- ▶ Have students read the words before stapling them to form a wall on the bulletin board.
- ▶ Invite students to write other words on bricks that they find challenging. Add these bricks to the wall. Encourage students to read the words daily.

57 ▷ Building Word Power ✂✂✂

Language Arts Standard ▶ Demonstrates understanding of multiple meaning words

- ▶ Prepare a bulletin board with the desired color of craft paper, a border, and the title "Building Word Power."
- ▶ Enlarge the carpenter (p. 176) and trace it on white craft paper. Color and cut out the figure.
- ▶ Staple the carpenter to the center of the bulletin board.
- ▶ Duplicate the word page (p. 178). Tell students to crease the sheet of paper along the center fold line.
- ▶ Invite students to choose a word that has more than one meaning. Have them write the word in a sentence on the outside of the folded paper and draw a picture that illustrates it.
- ▶ Have students underline the word.
- ▶ Tell students to open the sheet of paper and write the underlined word and two meanings in the spaces provided. Then have students write the correct letter of the meaning for the underlined word at the bottom.
- ▶ Have students crease the paper backward along the bottom fold line so the answer is concealed.
- ▶ Staple the opened papers to the bulletin board along the center crease. Then refold each paper so that the sentence and picture can be seen.
- ▶ Challenge students to read the sentences and meanings, guess the correct uses of the words, and check their answers.

Content-Related Bulletin Board Ideas
Math

58 ## How "Wood" You Order?

Math Standard ▶ **Compares and orders whole numbers**

▶ Prepare a bulletin board with the desired color of craft paper, a border, and the title "How 'Wood' You Order?"
▶ Enlarge the carpenter (p. 176) and trace it on white paper. Color the figure and cut it out. Staple it to the bulletin board.
▶ Duplicate a board (p. 176) for each student.
▶ Combine two sets of number cards 0 through 9 and invite students to choose two cards. Have them use these to write a two-digit number on a board.
▶ Tell students to cut out their boards.
▶ Challenge students to work cooperatively to make a plan to order all the numbers. Monitor students as they implement the plan.
▶ Staple the boards in numerical order on the bulletin board, according to the students' plan.

Social Studies

59 ## Handy Helpers

Social Studies Standard ▶ **Understands the importance of jobs**

▶ Prepare a bulletin board with the desired color of craft paper.
▶ Trace and cut out handprints (p. 177) using different colors of paper to make the border and a few templates.
▶ Staple the handprints along the sides and the top of the bulletin board to create a color pattern. Challenge students to continue the pattern around the bulletin board.
▶ Add the title "Handy Helpers."
▶ Enlarge the bricklayer (p. 177) and trace it on white craft paper. Color and cut it out. Staple the bricklayer to the bulletin board.
▶ Write *People use bricks to make buildings* on a sentence strip. Staple the sentence and a handprint next to the bricklayer.
▶ Invite students to draw a picture of someone in the community who does another important job. Have them dictate or write a sentence on a sentence strip describing the job.
▶ Have students use a template to trace a handprint on paper and cut it out.
▶ Staple the pictures, sentence strips, and handprints to the bulletin board in a pleasing arrangement.

Writing Process

60 ▶ Read All About It ✂✂✂

Language Arts Standard ▶ **Edits for appropriate grammar, spelling, and punctuation**

Materials

- newspaper boy pattern on page 179
- classified sections of the newspaper
- border
- white craft paper
- black construction paper
- writing paper
- scissors
- stapler
- pencils
- crayons or markers

Teacher Preparation

- ▶ Prepare a bulletin board with the classified sections of the newspaper, a border, and the title "Read All About It."
- ▶ Enlarge the newspaper boy (p. 179) on white craft paper to the desired size.
- ▶ Color and cut it out.
- ▶ Staple the newspaper boy to the middle of the bulletin board.
- ▶ Staple students' work in a pleasing arrangement on the bulletin board.

Student Directions

- ▶ Pick a topic from the newspaper to write about.
- ▶ Write a two- or three-sentence draft about the topic.
- ▶ Check your sentences for correct grammar, spelling, and punctuation.
- ▶ Rewrite the paper if necessary.
- ▶ Staple your writing paper to a sheet of black construction paper.

(page 18)

Additional Language Arts Bulletin Board Ideas

61 ▶ Hot off the Press ✂

Language Arts Standard ▶ Writes captions for illustrations

- ▶ Prepare a bulletin board with the desired color of craft paper.
- ▶ To prepare a border, collect several copies of the local newspaper. Then cut off the name of the newspaper, which is at the top of the front page. Staple the newspaper names around the bulletin board to make a border.
- ▶ Add the title "Hot off the Press."
- ▶ Invite students to draw a picture of a favorite story or a selected topic. Then have them dictate or write a sentence that tells about their illustration.
- ▶ Staple students' completed pictures in a pleasing arrangement on the bulletin board.

62 ▶ Letters to the Editor ✂✂

Language Arts Standard ▶ Writes in different forms for different purposes

- ▶ Prepare a bulletin board with the desired color of craft paper, a border, and the title "Letters to the Editor."
- ▶ Lead a discussion with students about the editorial page of the newspaper. Tell them that people write letters to express their opinion on many subjects and that their letters are printed in the newspaper for everyone to read.
- ▶ Read an appropriate letter from the editorial page of a newspaper to students.
- ▶ Invite students to write a letter to tell about something that they like to do. Have them use the greeting *Dear Editor*. Tell them that their letter will be placed on the bulletin board for everyone to read.
- ▶ Display students' completed letters on the bulletin board.

Content-Related Bulletin Board Ideas

63 ▶ Ads That Add Up

Math Standard ▶ Knows basic addition facts to 18

- Prepare a bulletin board with the desired color of craft paper, a border, and the title "Ads That Add Up."
- Cut out pictures of items such as food, clothing, jewelry, or tools from the four-color ad sections of a newspaper.
- Draw a plus sign in the centers of several sheets of paper. Glue different pictures on both sides of each plus sign. The total number of objects on the page should not be more than 18. For example, glue five pieces of jewelry on one side and eight shoes on the other side. Allow space at the bottom of the paper to write an equation.
- Laminate and staple the sheets of paper on the bulletin board.
- Invite students to use a washable marker to write the correct addition equation for each set of items. Have them ask a friend to check their answers.
- Have students use a damp paper towel to wipe their equations off of the sheets.

64 ▶ Delivering the News

Science Standard ▶ Records and compares collected information

- Prepare a bulletin board with the desired color of craft paper, a border, and the title "Delivering the News."
- Provide students with the materials necessary to conduct a selected science experiment.
- Duplicate the newspaper (p. 180) for each student. Have them record their science experiment results on the newspaper. Invite them to draw a picture of their results in the space provided.
- Staple students' newspapers in a pleasing arrangement on the bulletin board.

65 ▶ People in the News

Social Studies Standard ▶ Identifies leaders in the community, state, and nation

- Prepare a bulletin board with the desired color of craft paper, a border, and the title "People in the News."
- Cut out pictures of current leaders from a newspaper or magazine. Include pictures such as the President, Vice President, governor, and the mayor. Glue the pictures on construction paper. Place one side of hook and loop fastener tape at the bottom of each picture. Staple the pictures on the bulletin board.
- Write the name and position of each person on a sentence strip. Stick the other side of the hook and loop fastener tape on the back of the sentence strips.
- Invite students to correctly match the names, titles, and pictures.

Computation

66 ## Horsing Around with Number Sentences ✂

Math Standard ▶ **Models and creates addition and subtraction problems in real situations with concrete objects**

Materials

horse pattern on page 158, barn pattern on page 181, green craft paper, red craft paper, border, overhead projector, white construction paper, construction paper, sentence strips, self-stick adhesive tape, scissors, stapler, crayons or markers, index cards

Teacher Preparation

▶ Prepare a bulletin board with green craft paper, a border, and the title "Horsing Around with Number Sentences."

▶ Enlarge the barn (p. 181) and trace it on red craft paper. Cut it out and staple it in a corner near the top of the bulletin board.

▶ Draw a large corral with an open gate in the center of the bulletin board.

▶ Duplicate a horse (p. 158) on white construction paper for each student.

▶ Make five pockets by folding sentence strips lengthwise. Staple one pocket under the corral, one under the open gate, and one to the far right. Staple the remaining pockets under the barn.

▶ Place two sets of cards numbered 1–5 in one of the pockets under the barn.

▶ Place five horses in the second pocket under the barn each day so that all the students' horses are used over the course of a week.

▶ Invite students to use the horses to tell addition and subtraction stories, moving the horses in and out of the corral. Have students use the number cards to show the math problem in the pockets under the corral and gate. Have students place the answer to the story in the pocket to the far right.

Student Directions

▶ Cut out and color a horse.

▶ Put self-stick adhesive tape on the back of the horse.

▶ Make up an addition or subtraction problem using only the numbers 1–5.

(page 19)

Additional Math Bulletin Board Ideas

67 ► Look for "Sum" "Differences" in ✄✄ This Herd

Math Standard ► **Creates addition and subtraction problems and writes number sentences**

- ► Prepare a bulletin board with green craft paper, a border, and the title "Look for 'Sum' 'Differences' in This Herd."
- ► Enlarge the barn (p. 181) and trace it on red craft paper. Cut it out and staple it to the bulletin board.
- ► Duplicate the cow (p. 182) so that each student has several.
- ► Choose a number to be a sum or difference answer. For younger students, choose a number less than 18. For older students, choose a three-digit number.
- ► Write the number on an index card and identify it as the *sum* or *difference*. Attach the card to the barn door with self-stick adhesive tape.
- ► Have students color and cut out their cows.
- ► Challenge students to write a number sentence on the cow that uses the operation and the answer shown on the barn. Staple the completed cows to the bulletin board close together to make a herd.
- ► Change the number and operation several times during the week.

68 ► It's Time to Plant! ✄✄✄

Math Standard ► **Applies multiplication facts using concrete models**

- ► Prepare a bulletin board with brown craft paper, a border, and the title "It's Time to Plant!"
- ► Use a brown marker to make bumpy lines to represent a freshly plowed field.
- ► Enlarge the farmer (p. 181) and trace the figure on white craft paper. Color and cut out the farmer. Staple it to the bulletin board.
- ► Use dominoes with numbers to nine. Have each student select one domino.
- ► Tell students to use the two numbers on the domino to write a multiplication fact on the bottom of a sheet of brown paper.
- ► Then have students glue dried beans in an array on the brown paper that shows the fact.
- ► Staple students' papers to the bulletin board.

Content-Related Bulletin Board Ideas

69 ▶ Baa, Baa, Woolly Sheep

Science Standard ▶ Identifies characteristics of living organisms

- ▶ Prepare a bulletin board with the desired color of craft paper, a border, and the title "Baa, Baa, Woolly Sheep."
- ▶ Make several templates of the ear, nose, and tongue (p. 165) and cut them out.
- ▶ Have each student use a white crayon to trace two ears, three noses (two will be for the eyes), and one tongue on black paper. Have them cut out the parts and use the white crayon to add details to the eyes.
- ▶ Then have students glue cotton balls on a paper plate, covering the entire surface.
- ▶ Have students glue the eyes, ears, nose, and tongue cutouts on the cotton balls.
- ▶ Discuss the special characteristics of sheep with the class as you staple students' sheep to the bulletin board.

70 ▶ Old MacDonald Goes to Work

Social Studies Standard ▶ Understands the importance of jobs

- ▶ Prepare a bulletin board with the desired color of craft paper, a border, and the title "Old MacDonald Goes to Work."
- ▶ Enlarge the farmer (p. 181) and trace it on white craft paper. Color and cut out the farmer. Staple it to the bulletin board.
- ▶ Lead students in a discussion of all the jobs people do on a farm.
- ▶ Then have students imagine they are Old MacDonald. Have them write or dictate a sentence at the bottom of a sheet of white paper, telling about a job they would like to do if they were Old MacDonald. Have them draw a picture to go along with the sentence.
- ▶ Staple students' sentences and pictures to the bulletin board.

Classroom Management

71 ▶ Look at This "Moo-velous" Work!

- ▶ Prepare a bulletin board with the desired color of craft paper, a border, and the title "Look at This 'Moo-velous' Work!"
- ▶ Enlarge the cow (p. 182) on white craft paper and color it. Cut out the cow and staple it to the center of the bulletin board.
- ▶ Invite each student to display a paper of which they are proud.

Counting

72 ▷ Numbers by the Bunch ✂✂

Math Standard ▶ **Counts by 5s**

Materials

- blue, white, and green craft paper
- yellow construction paper
- banana pattern on page 183
- monkey pattern on page 183
- scissors
- stapler
- glue
- crayons or markers
- overhead projector
- adhesive notes

Teacher Preparation

▶ Cover the bulletin board with blue craft paper.

▶ Duplicate the banana (p. 183) to use as a template.

▶ Enlarge the monkey (p. 183) on the white craft paper.

▶ Color and cut out the monkey.

▶ Twist a narrow strip of green craft paper to resemble a vine. Make it the length of the bulletin board and staple it across the board. Cut out a few leaves from the green craft paper and staple them to the vine.

▶ Hang the monkey by its tail from the vine.

▶ Add the caption "Numbers by the Bunch."

▶ When students complete their bananas, staple the bunches around the edge of the bulletin board to make the border. Write the numbers *5, 10, 15, 20 . . .* on adhesive notes. Place the adhesive notes on the banana bunches as students count by 5s.

Student Directions

▶ Trace the banana template on the yellow construction paper five times.

▶ Cut out the five bananas.

▶ Glue them together at one end so that they resemble a bunch of bananas.

(page 19)

Note: Have each child make several bunches of bananas so that the border numbers go to at least 100.

Additional Math Bulletin Board Ideas

73 ▶ Swinging in Order ✂

Math Standard ▶ Orders numbers to 10

▶ Prepare a bulletin board with blue craft paper, a simple border. and the title "Swinging in Order."

▶ Twist a narrow strip of green craft paper to resemble a vine. Make it the length of the bulletin board and staple it across the board. Cut out a few leaves from the green craft paper and staple them to the vine.

▶ Duplicate a copy of the monkey (p. 183) for each student. Have students color and cut out the monkeys.

▶ Laminate the monkeys for durability and number the monkeys consecutively beginning with the number one.

▶ Have students hang the monkeys on the vine in numerical order.

74 ▶ Monkeying Around with Numbers ✂✂✂

Math Standard ▶ Orders numbers to 1,000

▶ Prepare a bulletin board with blue craft paper. Add a border and the title "Monkeying Around with Numbers."

▶ Enlarge the tree (p. 184) and make three, four, or five trees.

▶ Duplicate the banana (p. 183) several times to provide one for each student.

▶ Write *200–300* on the first tree, *500–600* on the second, and *900–1,000* on the third.

▶ Staple the trees on the bulletin board.

▶ Have students color and cut out the bananas. Laminate the bananas.

▶ Write the numbers *1–9* on each of three blank cubes.

▶ Invite students to roll the three number cubes one at a time and use those numbers to create a three-digit number. Have students use a washable marker to write the three-digit number on a banana.

▶ Challenge students to place their banana on the correct tree using a pushpin. If the number on the banana is not within the ranges shown on the trees, have students place the banana on the ground below the trees.

▶ To have students repeat the activity, use a spray bottle and paper towel to remove the numbers from the bananas.

Content-Related Bulletin Board Ideas

75 ▶ Here's the Scoop on the Troop

Language Arts Standard ▶ Produces rhyming words

- ▶ Prepare a bulletin board with the desired color of craft paper, a border, and the title, "Here's the Scoop on the Troop."
- ▶ Explain to students that a group of monkeys is called a troop.
- ▶ Enlarge the tree (p. 184) to make three trees.
- ▶ Write a target word family on each tree such as *frog, sled,* and *mat.* Staple the trees to the bulletin board.
- ▶ Duplicate a monkey (p. 183) for each student. Have students color and cut out the monkeys.
- ▶ Ask students to write a word on their monkey that rhymes with one of the target word families. Challenge each student to tape the monkey to the correct tree.
- ▶ Invite students to remove all of the monkeys from the trees. Then encourage them to take turns reading the words aloud and placing them back on the trees. Challenge each student to read a word that they did not write.

76 ▶ We Are Curious About Seeds

Science Standard ▶ Identifies external characteristics of plants

- ▶ Prepare a bulletin board with the desired color of craft paper, a border, and the title "We Are Curious About Seeds."
- ▶ Enlarge the monkey (p. 183), the tree (p. 184), and the magnifying glass (p. 199). Color and cut them out.
- ▶ Staple the monkey to the tree on the bulletin board.
- ▶ Staple the magnifying glass to monkey's hand.
- ▶ Have students examine seeds using a magnifying glass. Then have them draw a picture of the parts of a seed on a sheet of paper.
- ▶ Staple students' drawings on the bulletin board next to the tree.

Classroom Management

77 ▶ Going Bananas over Good Behavior

- ▶ Prepare a bulletin board with the desired color of craft paper, a border, and the title, "Going Bananas over Good Behavior."
- ▶ Enlarge the tree (p. 184). Color it and cut it out. Staple it to the bulletin board.
- ▶ Duplicate the monkey (p. 183) for each student to color and cut out.
- ▶ Have students name their own monkey and write its name on the monkey.
- ▶ Secure the monkeys along the bottom edge of the bulletin board with pushpins.
- ▶ As students demonstrate a selected skill or behavior, have them move their monkey up the tree.
- ▶ You may provide a small reward for a student when his or her monkey reaches the top of the tree.

Fractions

78 ▷ We're "Halving" a Colorful Cake! ✂✂

Math Standard ▶ Names fractional parts of a whole object when given a concrete representation

Materials

- cake pattern on page 187
- squares pattern on page 185
- craft paper
- border
- construction paper
- crayons or markers
- glue
- scissors
- stapler

Teacher Preparation

▶ Prepare a bulletin board with the desired color of craft paper, a border, and the title "We're 'Halving' a Colorful Cake!"

▶ Enlarge the cake (p. 187) and the joined squares (p. 185) to the same size. Use the joined squares to frame the squares on the cake.

▶ Color the top six squares of the cake one color and the bottom six squares a second color.

▶ Staple the cake to the bulletin board.

▶ Duplicate a cake for each student. Use the joined squares to trace the squares onto the cake.

▶ Tell students to imagine that the cake has two colors of frosting. Lead them in a discussion of halves. Help them realize that the squares could be cut apart and put back in any color order, but the cake would still show halves.

▶ Invite students to share their completed designs. Have them tell why the squares show halves before stapling them to the bulletin board.

Student Directions

▶ Choose two colors of crayons or markers. Color the top six squares of the cake with one color. Color the bottom six squares of the cake with another color.

▶ Tell a classmate why the cake shows halves.

▶ Cut the squares apart.

▶ Make a design with the squares. Glue the design on construction paper.

Extension: You may wish to have students use the cake and the joined squares to make designs showing thirds, fourths, sixths, and twelfths.

(page 20)

Additional Math Bulletin Board Ideas

79 ▸ Fair Share Foods ✂

Math Standard ▸ **Shares a whole by separating it in equal parts**

- ▸ Prepare a bulletin board with the desired color of craft paper, a border, and the title "Fair Share Foods."
- ▸ Cut out pictures of large food items from magazines. Make sure the foods are symmetrical and can be cut into halves, thirds, and/or fourths. Trim the edges of the picture so that only the food shows. (You may wish to make color copies of some of the foods.)
- ▸ Assign students to groups of two, three, or four.
- ▸ Give each group a food picture and tell students to cut it so that each person in the group gets an equal part. Have the members of the group glue the cut pieces on construction paper.
- ▸ To help students develop an awareness of a fraction name, invite the groups to explain how they cut the food and to identify the fractional parts.
- ▸ Staple each group's food pictures to the bulletin board.

80 ▸ It's a Pizza "Part-y"! ✂✂✂

Math Standard ▸ **Uses fraction names and symbols to describe fractional parts of whole objects with denominators less than 12**

- ▸ Prepare a bulletin board with white craft paper. Divide the entire paper into squares to look like a checkered tablecloth. Paint alternating squares red.
- ▸ Add a border and the title "It's a Pizza 'Part-y'!"
- ▸ Cut out balloon shapes and attach them to one edge of the bulletin board to make the board look three-dimensional. Add strings to the balloons.
- ▸ Make several templates of the pizza (p. 186).
- ▸ Invite students to use construction paper to make the perfect pizza. Tell them to trace the circumference of the template on white paper to make the pizza crust. Suggest they cut out a smaller red circle to represent the sauce.
- ▸ Encourage students to be creative as they cut out shapes or shred paper to make the toppings. Have them glue the layers together.
- ▸ Once the pizzas are dry, have students show how much of the pizza they can eat by themselves. Have them cut out that portion.
- ▸ Have students use the template pizza as a guide to identify the fractional part they ate and record it on the cut section.
- ▸ Challenge students to compare their fractions to other students' pizzas and to name equivalent fractions.
- ▸ After students share their pizza information, staple the pizzas to the bulletin board.

Content-Related Bulletin Board Ideas

81 ▶ We're Cooking Now!

Science Standard ▶ Identifies uses of heat to cause change

- ▶ Prepare a bulletin board with the desired color of craft paper, a border, and the title "We're Cooking Now!"
- ▶ Tell students to fold a sheet of paper in half. Have them open the paper and label one half *Before* and the other *After*.
- ▶ Ask them to think about their favorite hot food. Tell students to draw a picture of the food on the correct half of the paper showing the way it looks before it is cooked and after it is cooked.
- ▶ Have students write a sentence that tells how heat changes the food.
- ▶ Allow students to share their drawings and sentences before stapling them to the bulletin board.

82 ▶ Making a Cake Is a Farm "Product-ion"

Social Studies Standard ▶ Traces the development of a product from a natural resource to a finished product

- ▶ Prepare a bulletin board with the desired color of craft paper, a border, and the title "Making a Cake Is a Farm 'Product-ion'."
- ▶ Duplicate the cake (p. 187), farmer (p. 181), and cow (p. 182). Color them and cut them out. Staple them in a pleasing arrangement to the bulletin board.
- ▶ Find a recipe for making a cake from scratch. Write the recipe on chart paper.
- ▶ Collect containers of the ingredients for the cake, including flour and sugar bags, an egg carton, a vanilla bottle, a milk container, etc. Staple or attach the containers to the bulletin board along with the recipe on chart paper.
- ▶ Point out the different ingredients of the scratch cake to students and discuss how some people use a boxed cake mix instead.
- ▶ Assign students to groups and assign each group a food product that is on the bulletin board. Have groups research to find where the product comes from and some of the steps needed to process the food.
- ▶ Tell each group to write a brief report to share with the class.
- ▶ Staple the reports next to the containers on the bulletin board.

Graphs

83 ▸ Our Favorite Feathered Friends ✂

Math Standard ▸ Uses information from a graph of pictures in order to answer questions

Materials

- eagle pattern on page 189
- parrot pattern on page 189
- penguin pattern on page 189
- white craft paper
- border
- yardstick
- drawing paper
- individual photos of students
- self-stick adhesive tape
- scissors
- stapler
- crayons or markers

Teacher Preparation

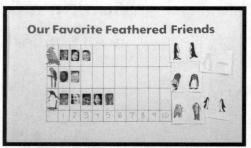

(page 20)

▸ Prepare a bulletin board with white craft paper, a border, and the title "Our Favorite Feathered Friends."

▸ Use a yardstick to draw a grid with four rows and eleven columns. Make the total width of the grid extend to the width of the bulletin board.

▸ Leaving the first square blank, write the numbers *1–10* in the squares in the bottom row.

▸ Duplicate the eagle, the parrot, and the penguin (p. 189). Enlarge them to fit the size of a square on the grid. Color and cut them out.

▸ Staple each bird in the first square of each row.

▸ Place self-stick adhesive tape on the back of the students' photos.

▸ Discuss which of the three birds is the class favorite.

▸ When students have completed their bird drawings, staple them around the graph in a pleasing design.

Student Directions

▸ Decide which of the three birds you like the best.

▸ Place your photo in a square of the row next to your favorite bird.

▸ Fold the drawing paper in half.

▸ Draw a picture of your favorite bird on the left side of the paper.

▸ Draw a picture of the class favorite on the right side of the paper.

▸ Write on the back of the picture if your favorite bird was the same or different from the class favorite.

Additional Bulletin Board Ideas

84 ▶ Birds Are New at the Zoo ✂✂

Math Standard ▶ Uses organized data to construct bar-type graphs

- ▶ Prepare a bulletin board with the desired color of craft paper, a border, and the title "Birds Are New at the Zoo."
- ▶ Duplicate and enlarge the birds (p. 189) so you have six owls, two eagles, seven parrots, five penguins, six flamingos, and four swans. Color them and cut them out. Staple them on the bulletin board in random order.
- ▶ Duplicate the blank grid (p. 188) for each student.
- ▶ Tell students that the zoo has just acquired these new birds. The zoo workers need to know how many of each kind of bird they have.
- ▶ Invite students to color a box in the graph for each type of bird displayed on the bulletin board.
- ▶ Staple students' graphs on the bulletin board in a pleasing design.

85 ▶ Coordinate the Coordinates ✂✂✂

Math Standard ▶ Solves problems by interpreting sets of data

- ▶ Prepare a bulletin board with the desired color of craft paper, a border, and the title "Coordinate the Coordinates."
- ▶ Use a yardstick to draw a grid in the middle of the bulletin board with nine rows and eight columns.
- ▶ Write the numbers *0–9* on the vertical axis of the grid. Write the numbers *0–8* on the horizontal axis of the grid.
- ▶ Write the bird names on the coordinates: *flamingos* (1, 7); *penguins* (2, 3); *owls* (3, 5); *eagles* (3, 8); *swans* (6, 7); *parrots* (7, 1).
- ▶ Write the coordinates only for each bird on an index card. Make multiple coordinate cards for each bird so that there is a card for each student.
- ▶ Place the cards in a library pocket and staple it to the bulletin board.
- ▶ Have students pick a card from the library pocket. Challenge students to use the coordinates to find the bird that is located there.
- ▶ Have students draw a picture on the card they picked of the bird that is located at the coordinates.
- ▶ Staple students' work on the bulletin board.

Content-Related Bulletin Board Ideas

86 ▸ The Name of the Game

Language Arts Standard ▸ **Knows the order of the alphabet**

- Prepare a bulletin board with the desired color of craft paper, a border, and the title "The Name of the Game."
- Write the 26 letters of the alphabet on small index cards. Staple the cards across the bottom of the bulletin board in alphabetical order.
- Cut construction paper into 4-inch x 4-inch squares. Place self-stick adhesive tape on the back of the paper squares.
- Write each bird name on a sentence strip: blue jay, canary, cardinal, flamingo, goldfinch, meadowlark, mockingbird, mallard duck, oriole, ostrich, parrot, penguin, roadrunner, robin, sea gull, sparrow, stork, woodpecker. Add other bird names if necessary.
- Give each student a sentence strip.
- Invite students to place a paper square above each letter on the bulletin board that is in their bird's name.
- When all of the bird names have been added to the graph, have students tell which letter of the alphabet appeared the most often and which appeared the least.

87 ▸ Dinner Time

Science Standard ▸ **Records and compares collected information**

- Prepare a bulletin board with the desired color of craft paper, a border, and the title "Dinner Time."
- Use a yardstick to draw a graph on the bulletin board with ten rows and five columns.
- Beginning at the bottom, write the numbers 1–10 on the left-hand side of each row of the graph.
- Below each column of the graph write *Day 1, Day 2, Day 3, Day 4,* and *Day 5.*
- Invite students to make a bird feeder using a mixture of two parts peanut butter with one part vegetable shortening. Have them cover a stale bagel with the peanut butter mixture and roll the bagel in birdseed. Then have students loop a piece of yarn through the bagel.
- Invite students to hang their bird feeders from trees or fences that are in various parts of the school grounds. Have students check their bird feeder each day for five days.
- Finally, have students write their name on a blank index card and place it on the graph above the day that their bird feeder was completely eaten.
- Discuss the results shown on the graph. Ask students if the location of their bird feeder affected how fast it was eaten.

Note: Be aware of students who may have food allergies.

Measurement

88 ▶ Going to Great Lengths to Catch Flies ✄✄✄

Math Standard ▶ **Selects and applies appropriate standard units and tools to measure length**

Materials

- frog pattern on page 190
- fly pattern on page 170
- blue and pink craft paper
- border
- green and gray construction paper
- writing paper
- rulers and yardsticks
- scissors
- stapler
- paper
- pencils

Teacher Preparation

Going to Great Lengths to Catch Flies

(page 21)

- ▶ Enlarge and duplicate six frogs (p. 190) on green construction paper and six flies (p. 170) on gray construction paper. Cut them out.
- ▶ Cover the bulletin board with blue craft paper.
- ▶ Add a border and the title "Going to Great Lengths to Catch Flies"
- ▶ Cut six long strips of pink craft paper for the frogs' tongues.
- ▶ Cut numbers 1–6 out of pink construction paper.
- ▶ Staple the frogs to the bulletin board so they look like they are jumping in all directions in a pond.
- ▶ Use a yardstick or ruler to measure a distance from each frog's mouth that is an exact increment of an inch, half inch, or one-fourth inch. Staple the fly at the exact measurement.
- ▶ Staple a pink strip between the frog's mouth and the fly.
- ▶ Staple a number next to each frog.
- ▶ Set rulers and yardsticks beside the bulletin board.
- ▶ Staple students' papers on the bulletin board.

Student Directions

- ▶ Number a sheet of paper from 1–6.
- ▶ Measure the length of each frog's tongue to the nearest one-fourth inch and record the number on your paper.

Additional Math Bulletin Board Ideas

89 ▸ Frog on a Log ✂

Math Standard ▸ **Recognizes the attributes of length**

- ▸ Cover a bulletin board with green craft paper. Add a border and the title "Frog on a Log."
- ▸ Cut out an irregular shape from blue craft paper to make a pond. Staple it to the bulletin board.
- ▸ Use scissors to fringe strips of green craft paper for grass and staple them to the green part of the bulletin board.
- ▸ Duplicate a frog (p. 190) on white paper for each student.
- ▸ Have students cut out the frogs. Invite students to use a sponge to paint a frog with green paint.
- ▸ Provide cards numbered 1–10. Then have students select a card.
- ▸ Tell them to write the number that is on the card on their frog. Have students join that many connecting cubes. Help students use chalk to trace the perimeter of the cubes on brown paper to represent a log. Have students cut out their logs.
- ▸ Tell students to glue their frog on the log.
- ▸ Challenge students to identify how many cubes long their log is before stapling their work to the bulletin board.
- ▸ You may wish to have partners compare the length of their logs and tell which is longer and which is shorter.

90 ▸ Lily Pad Leap ✂✂

Math Standard ▸ **Makes estimates**

- ▸ Prepare a bulletin board with blue craft paper, a border, and the title "Lily Pad Leap."
- ▸ Trace six frogs (p. 190) on dark green paper and six lily pads (p. 190) on light green paper. Cut them out.
- ▸ Write the letters *A–F* on the frogs and the numbers *1–6* on the lily pads. Staple the lily pads in a pleasing arrangement on the bulletin board.
- ▸ Students will estimate the distances between the lily pads and frogs, so write a different measurement in inches or feet on each lily pad. Staple a frog that distance from each lily pad.
- ▸ Challenge students to estimate which frog is the correct distance from each lily pad, according to the written measurement.
- ▸ Tell students to write the numbers *1–6* on a sheet of paper and write the corresponding letter of a frog that is on the bulletin board to show their estimates.
- ▸ Staple students' papers to the bulletin board.

Content-Related Bulletin Board Ideas

91 Hop to It, Frog!

Language Arts Standard ▶ Applies letter-sound correspondences

- ▶ Prepare a bulletin board with light blue craft paper, a border, and the title "Hop to It, Frog!"
- ▶ Enlarge the frog (p. 190) and trace it on green craft paper. Cut out the frog and staple it to the bulletin board.
- ▶ Enlarge and duplicate a lily pad (p. 190) on light green paper for each student.
- ▶ Have students cut out the lily pad and color a picture of something whose name contains either a short *o* sound or an *fr* blend. Vary the activity according to the grade level of the students.
- ▶ Staple the completed lily pads to the bulletin board in a pleasing arrangement.

92 Grow, Frog, Grow!

Science Standard ▶ Records changes in the life cycles of organisms

- ▶ Cover a bulletin board with blue craft paper. Add a border and the title "Grow, Frog, Grow!"
- ▶ Cut out four large arc-shaped arrows and staple them to the center of the bulletin board to form a frog life-cycle diagram.
- ▶ Make several templates of the long tadpole tail (p. 191), the short tadpole tail (p. 191), and the frog (p. 190).
- ▶ Have students follow the directions below to illustrate the life cycle of a frog.
- ▶ Staple the completed parts to the bulletin board to complete the diagram.

Egg Have students crumple a scrap of black paper and put it inside a resealable plastic bag. Have them blow air into the bag and seal it. Staple the bags to the bulletin board at the 12 o'clock position on the bulletin board. Place them close together to look like a mass of eggs.

Two tadpoles Have each student paint two bathroom-sized paper cups gray. While the cups dry, have students trace the two tails on gray paper and cut them out. Tell students to glue a tail inside each cup. Have them draw eyes and a mouth on the bottom of the cups to make the tadpoles' faces. Staple the long-tail tadpoles at the 3 o'clock position and the short-tail tadpoles at the 6 o'clock position.

Frog Have students trace a frog (p. 190) on green paper and cut it out. Then have them twist a pipe cleaner around a pencil to make a "spring," attaching one end of the spring to the back of the frog. Tell students to staple the other end of the pipe cleaner to the bulletin board at the 9 o'clock position. The frogs look like they are hopping as they move up and down on the "spring."

Money

93 ▶ How Much Is That Toy in the Window?

Math Standard ▶ **Determines the value of a collection of coins and bills**

Materials

toy patterns on page 201, money patterns on page 192, craft paper, border, sentence strips, small blank index cards, string, drawing paper, hole punch, scissors, stapler, glue, pencils, crayons or markers

Teacher Preparation

▶ Prepare a bulletin board with the desired color of craft paper, a border, and the title "How Much Is That Toy in the Window?"

▶ Cut paper the width of the bulletin board and scallop the bottom edge to resemble an awning on a store window. Staple it near the top of the bulletin board.

▶ Write math questions about the toys on sentence strips. Staple them in the center of the bulletin board.

▶ Enlarge the toys (p. 201) to the desired size. Color and cut them out. Staple them to the bulletin board.

▶ Fold sentence strips lengthwise and staple the ends to form a pocket for each toy.

▶ Punch a hole on the end of an index card. Tie a string through the hole to resemble a price tag. Staple a tag next to each toy. Write a money value on the tags.

▶ Duplicate several copies of the money (p. 192). Color them and cut them out.

▶ Make a money card for each toy. Glue dollars and coins on index cards that equal the value of the toys.

▶ Invite students to match the money cards and the price tags of equal value. Have students place the money cards in the pockets under the correct toys.

▶ Staple students' drawings on the bulletin board.

(page 21)

Student Directions

▶ Match the money cards and the price tags of equal value.

▶ Add the money values to answer the questions on the sentence strips.

▶ Draw and color a picture of your favorite toy.

Additional Math Bulletin Board Ideas

94 ▶ A Penny Is Just a Penny ✂

Math Standard ▶ Determines the value of a collection of coins

- ▸ Prepare a bulletin board with the desired color of craft paper, a border, and the title "A Penny Is Just a Penny."
- ▸ Enlarge and duplicate eight piggy banks (p. 193) and 30 pennies, 5 nickels, and one dime (p. 192). Color them and cut them out.
- ▸ Write a coin value on each of the piggy banks: 2¢, 3¢, 4¢, 5¢, 5¢, 10¢, 10¢, 10¢. Staple the banks to the bulletin board in a pleasing design.
- ▸ Place self-stick adhesive tape on the back of the coins.
- ▸ Have students name the coins.
- ▸ Invite students to place the correct coins on the piggy banks, matching the coin values written on the banks.
- ▸ Encourage students to think of two different ways to make five cents and three different ways to make ten cents.

95 ▶ Making "Cents" of It All ✂✂

Math Standard ▶ Determines the value of coins less than one dollar

- ▸ Prepare a bulletin board with the desired color of craft paper, a border, and the title "Making 'Cents' of It All."
- ▸ Duplicate the coin purse (p. 193) on lightweight white copy paper for each student. Have students color the top of the purse only and cut it out.
- ▸ Provide real coins that include pennies, nickels, dimes, and quarters.
- ▸ Have students think of a money amount less than a dollar to put in the coin purse. Then invite them to use a black crayon to make coin rubbings of that amount on their purse.
- ▸ Staple the coin purses on the bulletin board in a pleasing design.
- ▸ Have students write the coin values of their coin purses on blank index cards. Have them place self-stick adhesive tape to the backs of the cards.
- ▸ Challenge students to take turns placing the index cards on the correct purses.

Content-Related Bulletin Board Ideas

96 ▶ Bank on These Words

Language Arts Standard ▶ Identifies and sorts common words

- Prepare a bulletin board with the desired color of craft paper, a border, and the title "Bank on These Words."
- Enlarge and duplicate six piggy banks (p. 193). Color and cut them out.
- Write four words on each pig. Include three common words that are alike in some way and one that is different from the others, *e.g.,* penny, basket, dime, quarter; doll, bike, kite, fork.
- Staple the piggy banks on the bulletin board in a pleasing arrangement.
- Invite students to use a separate sheet of paper to write the three words on each piggy bank that belong together. Then have them write a word that tells how the other words are alike.
- Staple students' papers on the bulletin board.

97 ▶ A "Cents-able" Budget

Social Studies Standard ▶ Analyzes a simple budget that allocates money for spending and saving

- Prepare a bulletin board with the desired color of craft paper and the title "A 'Cents-able' Budget."
- Duplicate the money (p. 192) several times for each student. Have students color and cut them out. Staple the money around the bulletin board for the border.
- Make a copy of the money chart below and staple it in the middle of the bulletin board.
- Tell students that they have $50.00 and must use it in the ways described on the chart.
- Then explain that they have been invited by a friend to go to the movies. A movie ticket costs $6.00. Have them figure out if they will have enough money left over to go to the movies.
- Have students record their calculations on a sheet of paper.
- Staple their papers to the bulletin board.

How Far Does $50.00 Go?

1. Put one-fourth of your money in savings.
2. Buy your mother a plant that costs $6.31 for her birthday.
3. Buy a new notebook for $5.75.
4. Pay a late charge of $4.00 for a video game.
5. Buy a pair of skates for $12.98.

Patterns

98 ▶ Pesky Picnic Ants ✂

Math Standard ▶ Identifies, extends, and creates simple patterns

Materials

- big ant pattern on page 194
- small ant pattern on page 194
- white craft paper
- red paint
- border
- drawing paper

- scissors
- stapler
- glue
- pencils
- crayons or markers

Teacher Preparation

▶ Prepare a bulletin board with craft paper. Paint the craft paper with red horizontal and vertical stripes to give the bulletin board a checked appearance.

▶ Add a border and the title "Pesky Picnic Ants."

▶ Duplicate a generous supply of big and small ants (p. 194).

▶ When students have completed their drawings, staple them on the bulletin board in a pleasing arrangement.

Student Directions

▶ Draw a picture on drawing paper of a red and white checked picnic tablecloth with your favorite picnic food on it.

▶ Think of a simple size pattern sequence, *e.g.,* big, little, big, little or big, big, little.

▶ Color and cut out the ants needed to make your pattern sequence.

▶ Glue them around the edge of your picnic picture according to your pattern.

▶ Read your pattern aloud as it is stapled on the bulletin board.

(page 22)

Additional Math Bulletin Board Ideas

99 Flying Through Number Patterns ✂✂

Math Standard ▶ **Finds patterns in numbers such as in a 100s chart**

▶ Prepare a bulletin board with the desired color of craft paper, a border, and the title "Flying Through Number Patterns."

▶ Duplicate 50 ladybugs (p. 197), 10 butterflies (p. 194), and 20 bees (p. 206). Have students color and cut them out. Laminate the ladybugs and butterflies. Place a small piece of poster putty on the back of each insect.

▶ Duplicate three number charts (p. 195). Enlarge the charts so that the squares match the size of the insects. Laminate the charts. Then staple them evenly across the bulletin board at students' eye level.

▶ Challenge students to cover each number on a chart with a butterfly as they count by 10s. Next have them count by 5s using the bees to cover the numbers. Finally have students count by 2s using the ladybugs.

100 Bugs Can Be a Problem ✂✂✂

Math Standard ▶ **Uses patterns to solve problems**

▶ Prepare a bulletin board with the desired color of craft paper, a border, and the title "Bugs Can Be a Problem."

▶ Draw a horizontal line to divide the bulletin board in half.

▶ Duplicate 10 butterflies (p. 194). Enlarge them if desired. Color them all the same color and cut them out.

▶ Duplicate 20 ladybugs (p. 197), color them, and cut them out.

▶ Arrange the butterflies in a row on the top half of the bulletin board and the ladybugs in groups on the bottom half.

▶ Staple them according to the patterns below.

▶ Challenge students to draw a picture of what comes next in both patterns. Then have them write the rules for the patterns.

Note: The butterfly rule is that the head moves to the right in four turns, and the ladybug rule is the diagonal row increases by one ladybug.

▶ Staple students' completed work around the edge of the bulletin board.

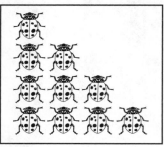

Content-Related Bulletin Board Ideas

101 Going Buggy Over VCE Words

Language Arts Standard ▶ Writes with more proficient spelling of regularly spelled patterns

- ▸ Prepare a bulletin board with the desired color of craft paper, a border, and the title "Going Buggy Over VCE Words."
- ▸ Enlarge and duplicate nine ladybugs (p. 196). Color and cut them out.
- ▸ Cut out nine pictures from magazines showing objects whose names have a **VCE** pattern. Glue each picture to an index card.
- ▸ Glue the picture cards on the ladybugs and staple them to the bulletin board in a pleasing arrangement.
- ▸ Invite students to use the **VCE** pattern to write the picture names on a separate sheet of paper.
- ▸ Provide students with a paper plate. Have them decorate the plate to resemble a ladybug.
- ▸ Staple students' ladybugs and completed papers around the edge of the bulletin board.

Note: A word with a **VCE** pattern has a vowel, consonant, *e* combination, resulting in a long vowel sound.

102 From Egg to Butterfly Growth Patterns

Science Standard ▶ Observes and identifies growth patterns

- ▸ Prepare a bulletin board with the desired color of craft paper, a border, and the title "From Egg to Butterfly Growth Patterns."
- ▸ Duplicate the butterfly (p. 194) for each student. Have students color and cut out the butterflies.
- ▸ Then have students draw lines on a paper plate to divide it into four equal sections.
- ▸ Challenge students to research the life cycle of a butterfly in a book or on the Internet. Lead a discussion with students about the stages of the insect's life cycle and about how it is repeated.
- ▸ Invite students to write the words *egg, larva, pupa,* and *adult* in each section of their plate.
- ▸ Have them draw a picture of the egg, larva, and pupa stages of the butterfly life cycle in the correct section.
- ▸ Next have them glue their butterfly on the adult section of the plate.
- ▸ Staple students' paper plates on the bulletin board.

Probability

103 The Tile Game ✂✂✂

Math Standard ▶ Predicts the probability of outcomes of simple experiments and tests the predictions

Materials

- 4 red and 4 blue tiles
- red and blue construction paper
- yellow craft paper
- border
- sentence strips
- white lunch bag
- tape
- scissors
- stapler
- envelope

Teacher Preparation

▶ Prepare a bulletin board with yellow craft paper, a border, and the title "The Tile Game."

▶ Staple the bag to one side of the bulletin board. Put the red and blue tiles in it.

▶ Staple five sentence strips, one on top of the other, to the right of the bag.

▶ Cut out a generous supply of two-inch squares from red and blue paper. Keep these in an envelope.

▶ Show students eight of the tiles in the bag. Lead them in a discussion of what they think will happen if individual tiles are pulled out, the colors are recorded, the tiles are returned to the bag each time. Introduce the terms *probability, certain, equally likely,* and *impossible.*

▶ Using the selection of a tile as a reward for positive behavior. Allow students to draw a tile from the bag and record the color by stapling or taping a corresponding paper square to a sentence strip. Allow ten squares per strip. After each addition, lead students in a discussion of what is happening and what they predict will happen. Once fifty squares have been stapled to the bulletin board, discuss the results and compare the data to students' predictions.

(page 22)

Additional Math Bulletin Board Ideas

104 ▶ Gum Ball Guessing ✄

Math Standard ▶ Identifies events as likely or unlikely

- Prepare a bulletin board with white craft paper.
- Make several templates of the circle (p. 202).
- Choose five colors of construction paper and cut out multiple circles from each color. Use the circles to make a patterned border along the sides and top of the bulletin board.
- Add the title "Gum Ball Guessing."
- Enlarge the gum ball dispenser (p. 197) and trace five of them on craft paper, matching the five colors in the border. Cut out the dispensers so that only the frame shows. Staple the dispensers to the bulletin board in a pleasing design.
- Tell students to choose one of the five colors of construction paper, trace a circle, and cut it out to make a gumball.
- Have students share their gum ball color with the class. Help them tape their gum balls inside the matching dispenser.
- Discuss with students which color gum ball is likely or unlikely to drop from each dispenser.
- Invite students to help complete the patterned border along the bottom of the bulletin board by tracing, cutting out, and staping additional circles.

105 ▶ Ready! Set! Roll! ✄✄

Math Standard ▶ Discusses events related to students' experiences as likely or unlikely

- Prepare a bulletin board with white craft paper.
- Enlarge the road (p. 198) and trace the scene on the bulletin board. Paint it.
- Add a border and the title "Ready! Set! Roll!"
- Place two small cars near the bulletin board.
- Ask several questions, such as *Which is likely to be the longest path to the park? Which two paths are likely the same length?* and *Which path is unlikely to go to the park?* Challenge students to choose one question to answer and solve it by rolling the cars along the paths.

Content-Related Bulletin Board Ideas

106 "Bubble-icious" Blends

Language Arts Standard ▶ Recognizes letter-sound correspondences including consonant blends

▸ Prepare a bulletin board with white craft paper. Add a border and the title "'Bubble-icious' Blends."
▸ Make several templates of the circle (p. 202).
▸ Enlarge the gum ball dispenser (p. 197) and trace several on white craft paper. Color the frames.
▸ Write a target blend on the top of each dispenser.
▸ Invite students to trace and cut out construction paper circles to make gum balls.
▸ Challenge them to draw pictures on the gum balls of objects whose names contain the target blends. Or invite them to write words that have the target blends.
▸ Help students staple the gum balls to the corresponding dispenser.

107 "Wheel-y" Fun Facts

Math Standard ▶ Knows basic addition facts to 18

▸ Prepare a bulletin board with white craft paper.
▸ Enlarge the road (p. 198) and trace the scene on the bulletin board. Paint it.
▸ Add a border and the title "'Wheel-y' Fun Facts."
▸ Write the numbers *1–18* on index cards.
▸ Ask students to draw a race car that can be stapled to the bulletin board.
▸ Have them choose a card and write that number on the car door.
▸ Tell students to write a pair of addends on the tires that equal the race car number.
▸ Help students staple the cars to the bulletin board.

Classroom Management

108 Sticking to Good Behavior

▸ Prepare a bulletin board with white craft paper, a border, and the title "Sticking to Good Behavior."
▸ Enlarge the gum ball dispenser (p. 197) and trace it on the bulletin board. Color the frame of the dispenser.
▸ Staple stickers attached to their backings inside the gum ball machine.
▸ When students exhibit positive behavior, allow them to select a sticker from the gum ball machine.

Problem Solving

109 Clue Us In! ✂✂✂

Math Standard ▶ Uses a problem-solving model that incorporates understanding the problem, making a plan, carrying out the plan, and evaluating the solution

Materials

footstep pattern on page 200, detective pattern on page 199, magnifying glass pattern on page 199, white craft paper, overhead projector, black and white construction paper, writing paper, pencils, scissors, stapler, crayons or markers, craft paper

Teacher Preparation

▶ Prepare a bulletin board with the desired color of craft paper and the title "Clue Us In!"

▶ Use a white crayon to trace the footsteps (p. 200) multiple times on black construction paper. Cut the footsteps out and use them as the border.

▶ Enlarge the detective (p. 199) and trace it on white craft paper. Color the figure and cut it out. Staple it on the bulletin board.

▶ Duplicate three magnifying glasses (p. 199) on white paper. Color the frames black and cut them out. Write three clues on the magnifying glasses: *The number is even. The number has three digits. The number's digits equal 15.* Staple the glasses to the detective's hand.

▶ Make several templates of the magnifying glass.

▶ Staple students' completed work on the bulletin board.

Student Directions

▶ Read the clues on the bulletin board. Write ten numbers that will answer the clues on a sheet of paper.

▶ Think of one last clue that will solve the number mystery.

▶ Trace a magnifying glass on black construction paper and cut it out.

▶ Cut out a circle from white paper that is the same shape as the glass part of the magnifying glass. Write your final clue on the white circle.

▶ Use a white crayon to write the number answer in the center of the magnifying glass.

▶ Place the white circle with the clue on top of the answer. Staple once to make a lift-up flap.

(page 23)

Bulletin Boards, SV 1-4190-1884-1

Additional Math Bulletin Board Ideas

110 Toying Around with Problems ✂

Math Standard ▶ Sorts objects by an attribute

- ▶ Prepare a bulletin board with white craft paper.
- ▶ Enlarge the detective (p. 199) and trace it on one side of the bulletin board.
- ▶ Enlarge the eight toys (p. 201) and trace them beside the detective in a pleasing arrangement.
- ▶ Color all the figures.
- ▶ Add a border and the title "Toying Around with Problems."
- ▶ Duplicate the page with the toys (p. 201) for each student.
- ▶ Challenge students to help the detective sort the toys into different groups. Have them color and cut out the toys and glue them on paper to show the groups.
- ▶ Before stapling students' papers to the bulletin board, have students tell the criteria for each group classification.

111 Fishing for Numbers ✂✂

Math Standard ▶ Develops an appropriate problem-solving strategy

- ▶ Prepare a bulletin board with white craft paper. Add a border and the title "Fishing for Numbers."
- ▶ Enlarge the detective (p. 199) and trace it on one side of the bulletin board. Color the detective.
- ▶ Enlarge the aquarium (p. 200) and trace it beside the detective.
- ▶ Make several templates of the small fish (p. 153).
- ▶ Invite students to trace a fish on their favorite color of construction paper and cut it out. Help them staple the fish in a pleasing arrangement inside the aquarium.
- ▶ Tell students to help the detective show how many of each color of fish are in the aquarium. Provide art supplies and paper and encourage students to be creative.
- ▶ Invite students to share their ideas before stapling their completed work to the bulletin board.

Content-Related Bulletin Board Ideas

112 The Case of the Missing Letters

Language Arts Standard ▶ Knows the order of the alphabet

- Prepare a bulletin board with the desired color of craft paper. Add a border and the title "The Case of the Missing Letters."
- Enlarge the detective (p. 199) and trace the figure on white craft paper. Color the detective and cut it out. Staple the figure to the bulletin board.
- Trace a magnifying glass (p. 199) on white paper, color the frame black, and cut it out. Staple the magnifying glass to the detective's hand.
- Staple an envelope to one corner of the bulletin board.
- Staple letter cutouts in alphabetical order to the bulletin board, leaving out five or six letters. Leave space to show where letters are missing. Place a piece of self-stick adhesive tape in each space.
- Put the missing letters in the envelope.
- Invite students to solve the case by attaching the letters where they belong.

113 Take a Closer Look at Your World

Science Standard ▶ Collects information using tools

- Prepare a bulletin board with the desired color of craft paper, a border, and the title "Take a Closer Look at Your World."
- Enlarge the magnifying glass (p. 199) and trace several on white craft paper. Color the frames black and cut them out. Staple them to the bulletin board.
- Gather interesting items related to a topic of study and put them in resealable bags. Staple one bag to the center of each magnifying glass.
- Place real magnifying glasses near the bulletin board. Invite students to use the tools to observe the items.
- During group time, lead students in a discussion about their observations.

114 Steps to Good Citizenship

Social Studies Standard ▶ Identifies characteristics of good citizenship

- Prepare a bulletin board with the desired color of craft paper, a border, and the title "Steps to Good Citizenship."
- Enlarge and trace the newspaper boy (p. 179) on white craft paper. Color and cut it out. Staple the figure on the bulletin board.
- Make several templates of the footstep (p. 200). Invite students to trace a footstep on black paper and cut it out.
- Have them use a white crayon to write things they can do to be good citizens.
- Staple the footsteps on the bulletin board so they look like they create a diagonal path from the lower left-hand corner to the upper right-hand corner.

Shapes

115 Open the Door for Shapes ✂✂

Math Standard ▶ Identifies attributes of any shape or solid

Materials

- circle pattern (p. 202)
- car pattern (p. 202)
- blue and brown craft paper
- border
- black construction paper
- brads
- scissors
- stapler
- pencils
- crayons or markers

Teacher Preparation

▶ Prepare a bulletin board with blue and brown craft paper to resemble hills and sky. Draw a curved road across the brown hills.

▶ Add a border and the title "Open the Door for Shapes."

▶ Make several templates of the circle (p. 202). Cut them out.

▶ Duplicate the car (p. 202) for each student.

▶ When students have completed their cars, staple them on the road in a pleasing arrangement.

▶ Write a shape clue on the door of each car, such as *I have four equal sides* or *A ball is shaped like me.*

▶ Draw pictures of the answers on the inside of the car doors.

Student Directions

▶ Color and cut out the car.

▶ Cut the broken line and fold open the car door.

▶ Trace the circle template on black construction paper twice and cut out the two circles.

▶ Use brads to attach the two circles on the car as wheels.

▶ Read the clues on the cars and answer with the names of shapes. Peek inside the doors to check your answers.

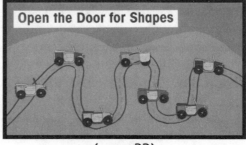

(page 23)

Additional Math Bulletin Board Ideas

116 Sailing Along with Shapes ✂

Math Standard ▶ **Combines geometric shapes to make new geometric shapes**

- Prepare a bulletin board with the desired color of craft paper. Add a border and the title "Sailing Along with Shapes."
- Duplicate a generous supply of triangles, circles, and squares (p. 202).
- Provide students with sheets of blue construction paper.
- Challenge them to build a sailboat using the shapes.
- Then have students glue their sailboat on the blue paper.
- Staple the sailboats to the bulletin board in a pleasing arrangement.

117 Trucks Only in This Area ✂✂✂

Math Standard ▶ **Uses concrete models of square units to determine the area of shapes**

- Prepare a bulletin board with the desired color of craft paper, a border, and the title "Trucks Only in This Area."
- Enlarge the truck (p. 203) and provide a copy for each student. Have them color it and cut it out.
- Cut a generous supply of one-inch paper squares.
- Invite students to completely cover the trailer section of the truck with one-inch paper squares, laying the squares side by side and not overlapping.
- Challenge students to count the squares to find the area of the trailer.
- Have students remove the squares and write a sentence on the trailer that tells the area of the truck. For example, students can write *My truck is __ square inches.*
- Staple students' completed trucks in a pleasing arrangement on the bulletin board.

Content-Related Bulletin Board Ideas

118 Stay on Track with Contractions

Language Arts Standard ▶ **Writes with more proficient spelling of contractions**

- ▶ Prepare a bulletin board with the desired color of craft paper, a border, and the title "Stay on Track with Contractions."
- ▶ Enlarge the engine (p. 159), the caboose (p. 203), and ten boxcar patterns (p. 203). Color and cut them out. Staple the train cars on the bulletin board.
- ▶ Write the following words on each of the boxcars: *is not, they are, have not, we are, I am, did not, it is, you are, cannot, who is.*
- ▶ Have students read the words on each car. Then have them write the contractions for the words on a separate sheet of paper and use them in sentences.
- ▶ Display students' completed papers on the bulletin board.

119 On The Road Again

Social Studies Standard ▶ **Locates communities and states or provinces on maps**

- ▶ Prepare a bulletin board with the desired color of craft paper, a border, and the title "On the Road Again."
- ▶ Cover the bulletin board with a large national road map. Highlight the major highways on the map.
- ▶ Write simple directions such as the ones listed below on sentence strips.
  - Start in Chicago, Illinois, and go to Salt Lake City, Utah.
  - Start in Seattle, Washington, and go to Los Angeles, California.
  - Start in Washington, D.C., and go to Atlanta, Georgia.
  - Start in St. Paul, Minnesota, and go to Tulsa, Oklahoma.
- ▶ Staple an envelope to the bulletin board to hold the direction cards.
- ▶ Invite students to put their finger on the starting point and follow the highway to get to their destination.

Classroom Management

120 Shape Up!

- ▶ Prepare a bulletin board with the desired color of craft paper, a border, and the title "Shape Up!"
- ▶ Enlarge the circle, triangle, and square (p. 202) on different colors of poster board. Cut them out. Then cut each shape into several pieces, making a puzzle.
- ▶ Invite students to use self-stick adhesive tape to add a puzzle piece each time a designated behavior is observed.
- ▶ Discuss a reward or an activity that they will earn when the puzzles are completed.

Sorting and Classifying

121 ▷ I Can Sort, Too. I Can. I Can. ✂✂✂

Math Standard ▶ **Identifies and sorts solid geometric shapes**

Materials

- gingerbread man pattern on page 204
- cards on page 205
- blue and brown craft paper
- overhead projector
- sentence strips
- crayons or markers
- glue
- scissors
- stapler
- border

Teacher Preparation

- ▶ Cover the bulletin board with blue craft paper.
- ▶ Enlarge five gingerbread men (p. 204) on the brown craft paper.
- ▶ Draw a face on each gingerbread man. Then cut them out and laminate them.
- ▶ Duplicate the geometric solids picture cards (p. 205). Color and cut out the cone, cylinder, cube, rectangular prism, and the sphere. Glue one picture on each gingerbread man.
- ▶ Staple the gingerbread men on the bulletin board.
- ▶ Cut a sentence strip in half. Fold the piece lengthwise. Staple each end of the strip to the bulletin board to form a pocket. Place one below each gingerbread man.
- ▶ Add the title "I Can Sort, Too. I Can, I Can." and a border.
- ▶ Color and cut out and laminate the remaining pictures that are examples of geometric solids.

Student Directions

- ▶ Sort and name the pictures of the geometric shapes.
- ▶ Place each picture in the pocket below the gingerbread man that has that shape.

(page 24)

Additional Math Bulletin Board Ideas

122 Baking with Color ✂

Math Standard ▶ Sorts objects by colors

- ▶ Prepare a bulletin board with the desired color of craft paper, a border, and the title "Baking with Color."
- ▶ Make four cookie sheets by covering a half sheet of poster board with foil. Staple them in a pleasing arrangement on the bulletin board.
- ▶ Duplicate the gingerbread man (p. 204) on red, yellow, blue, and green construction paper for each student. Have students cut out and decorate their four gingerbread men.
- ▶ Invite students to sort the gingerbread men by colors.
- ▶ Help students staple the gingerbread men on the cookie sheets by colors.

123 Sort, Sort, As Fast as You Can ✂✂

Math Standard ▶ Sorts objects using two attributes

- ▶ Prepare the bulletin board with the desired color of craft paper, a border, and the title "Sort, Sort, As Fast as You Can."
- ▶ Draw three large circles on the bulletin board. Place several pushpins in each circle.
- ▶ Then write one of the following sentences below each circle: *My buttons are square with four holes. My buttons are round with two holes. My buttons are square with two holes.*
- ▶ Duplicate the gingerbread man (p. 204) for each student. Have students color and cut out their gingerbread man.
- ▶ Punch a hole at the top of each gingerbread man.
- ▶ Duplicate enough buttons (p. 204) so that each student has one button. Have students glue one button on their gingerbread man.
- ▶ Hide the gingerbread men around the room.
- ▶ Tell students that the gingerbread men have run away. Invite them to find the gingerbread men.
- ▶ As each gingerbread man is found, have students hang it on a pushpin in the circle that has the correct attributes.

Content-Related Bulletin Board Ideas

124   Catch Me If You Can

Language Standard ▶ Recognizes letter-sound correspondences including consonant digraphs

▶ Prepare the bulletin board with the desired color of craft paper, a border, and the title "Catch Me If You Can."

▶ Duplicate two copies of the gingerbread man (p. 204) on brown construction paper for each target digraph. Decorate, cut out, and laminate them.

▶ Write the target digraphs on one set of gingerbread men. Tape one end of a piece of yarn on the back of each one. Staple the gingerbread men in a column on the left side of the bulletin board and let the yarn hang freely.

▶ Cut out pictures from magazines of objects whose names match each target digraph. Glue the pictures on the second set of gingerbread men. Staple these gingerbread men in a column on the right side of the bulletin board in random order.

▶ Have students tape the yarn from the target digraphs to the correct pictures.

▶ Challenge students by rearranging the order of the gingerbread men in the right column.

125   Running North, South, East, or West

Social Studies Standard ▶ Uses the four cardinal directions

▶ Prepare the bulletin board with the desired color of craft paper, a border, and the title "Running North, South, East, or West."

▶ Draw a star in the center of the bulletin board.

▶ Duplicate a gingerbread man (p. 204) for each student. Reduce or enlarge the pattern to the desired size. Draw four paths from the star to the edge of the bulletin board with six stepping stones on each path. Make the stones the size of the gingerbread men and make the paths go north, south, east, and west.

▶ Provide one die and one blank cube. On the blank cube, write one of the four cardinal directions (*N, E, W,* and *S*) on each side of the cube. Repeat a direction on the two remaining sides.

▶ Have students color and cut out the gingerbread man.

▶ Tell students to place their gingerbread man on the star with self-stick adhesive tape.

▶ Invite students to roll the die and the cube.

▶ Have students move their gingerbread man the number of spaces indicated on the die and in the direction indicated on the cube. Have students tape their gingerbread men where they land.

▶ Discuss where each gingerbread man lands.

Time

126 It's Time to Get "Buzzy"!

Math Standard ▶ **Tells time to the hour and half hour**

Materials

- bee pattern on page 206
- hive cell pattern on page 206
- clock face pattern on page 207
- blue and yellow craft paper
- border
- yellow and white construction paper
- overhead projector
- self-stick adhesive tape
- scissors
- crayons or markers
- glue
- stapler

Teacher Preparation

▶ Prepare a bulletin board with blue craft paper, a border, and the title "It's Time to Get 'Buzzy'!"

▶ Enlarge a bee (p. 206) and trace it on yellow craft paper. Color the stripes black and cut out the bee. Staple the bee to one side of the bulletin board.

▶ Duplicate a bee (p. 206) and hive cell (p. 206) on yellow construction paper for each student.

▶ Duplicate the clock face (p. 207) on white construction paper for each student.

▶ Make a pocket by cutting a sentence strip the length of the smaller bees and folding it lengthwise. Staple each end of the strip to the corner of the bulletin board.

▶ When students complete the hive cells, staple them together to form a comb.

(page 24)

▶ Put a piece of self-stick adhesive tape beside each clock face.

▶ Put the bees in the pocket.

▶ Challenge students to match the bees to the times on the clocks.

Student Directions

▶ Cut out a hive, bee, and clock face.

▶ Color the bee's stripes black.

▶ Write a time to the hour or half hour on the bee.

▶ Draw hands on the clock to show the time you wrote on the bee.

▶ Glue the clock face to the center of a hive cell.

102

Additional Math Bulletin Board Ideas

127 We Are Busy Bees! ✂

Math Standard ▶ Reads a calendar

- ▶ Prepare a bulletin board with the desired color of craft paper, a border, and the title "We Are Busy Bees!"
- ▶ Draw the month's calendar in the center of the bulletin board.
- ▶ Duplicate a generous supply of bees (p. 206) on yellow paper in a size that fit the calendar's squares. Color the bees' stripes and cut them out.
- ▶ Write dates and a brief description of special activities on the bees, such as days the class will visit the library, students' birthdays, and field trips.
- ▶ Gather students around the calendar and discuss its parts, including the month, days, and dates.
- ▶ Invite volunteers to help find where each bee belongs on the calendar and staple it to the date.

128 Handy Clock Advice for Busy Bees ✂✂✂

Math Standard ▶ Tells time on analog and digital clocks

- ▶ Prepare a bulletin board with the desired color of craft paper, a border, and the title "Handy Clock Advice for Busy Bees."
- ▶ Enlarge the bee (p. 206) on yellow craft paper, color the stripes black, and cut it out. Staple it to the bulletin board.
- ▶ Draw dashed lines around the bulletin board to give the impression that the bee is flying.
- ▶ Duplicate the clock face (p. 207) and the digital clock (p. 207) many times on white paper. Cut out the clocks.
- ▶ Create a code in which a time represents a letter of the alphabet in a saying, such as Bee on Time, Time Flies, or Clocks Have Helping Hands. For example, you may have 2:16 stand for the letter *B* and 9:45 stand for the letter *E*.
- ▶ Write a time with numbers on the digital clock and the letter for which it stands. Then draw the hands on the clock face to show the same time. Repeat this procedure for each letter in the saying.
- ▶ Staple the clock faces at the top of the bulletin board in the order of the letters in the saying and the digital clocks along the bottom of the bulletin board.
- ▶ Challenge students to decipher the code.

Content-Related Bulletin Board Ideas

129　A Busy Word Hive

Language Standard ▶ Demonstrates understanding of synonyms

- Prepare a bulletin board with blue craft paper, a border, and the title "A Busy Word Hive."
- Enlarge a bee (p. 206) and trace it on yellow craft paper. Color the stripes black and cut out the bee. Staple the bee on one side of the bulletin board.
- Duplicate several bees (p. 206) and one hive cell (p. 206) on yellow construction paper for each student. Have students cut out the bees and the hive cell and color the bees' stripes black.
- Make a pocket by cutting a sentence strip the length of the smaller bees and folding it lengthwise. Staple the bottom and sides, and then staple the pocket to the corner of the bulletin board.
- Write words on students' completed hives that have synonyms. Staple the hive cells together to form a comb on the bulletin board.
- Use as many bees as possible to write several synonyms for each word. Put a piece of self-stick adhesive tape on the back of each bee.
- Challenge students to match the bees to the correct hives.

130　Get the Facts on Bees

Math Standard ▶ Recalls and applies basic facts

- Prepare a bulletin board with the desired color of craft paper, a border, and the title "Get the Facts on Bees."
- Reduce the hive cell (p. 206) and cut out several templates. Have students use a template to draw hive cells that cover a sheet of yellow construction paper, forming a comb.
- Duplicate a bee (p. 206) on yellow paper for each student. Have students cut out a bee and color the stripes black.
- Provide a set of number cards with the numbers 1–9. Have students select a number, write that number on the bee, and return the number card to the set.
- Depending on the skill level of the students, tell them to write a different addition, subtraction, or multiplication fact with the chosen number in each hive cell.
- Have students glue their completed bees to the comb on the bulletin board.

Animals

131 Do You ... Hibernate? Migrate? Adapt? ✂✂✂

Science Standard ▶ **Classifies organisms on properties and patterns**

Materials

- craft paper
- border
- index cards
- yardstick
- markers or crayons
- resource books about animals
- pencils
- stapler

Teacher Preparation

▶ Prepare a bulletin board with the desired color of craft paper.

▶ Use a yardstick to draw a horizontal line about 12 inches from the top. Add the title "Do You ..."

▶ Draw two vertical lines that divide the rest of the bulletin board into three equal columns. Add the headings "Hibernate? Migrate? Adapt?"

▶ Add a border.

▶ Write the name of an animal that sleeps, moves, or changes on an index card. Consider the following animals: sleeps—bear, snake, raccoon, groundhog, skunk, frog; moves—bat, worm, goose, butterfly, whale; changes—reindeer, beaver, mouse, fox, rabbit, mole.

▶ Have each student select a card.

▶ Have students identify the animal they drew and read their sentence about what the animal does during the winter. Have students staple their completed cards in the correct column.

Student Directions

▶ Choose a card with an animal name. Find information about what the animal does during the winter months.

▶ Draw and color a picture of that animal on the card.

▶ Write a sentence on the card that tells what the animal does during the winter months.

(page 25)

Additional Science Bulletin Board Ideas

132 Feathers, Fur, or Scales ✀

Science Standard ▶ Identifies characteristics of living organisms

- Use three colors of craft paper to divide a bulletin board into three diagonal parts. Add a border.
- Write the words for the title "Feathers, Fur, or Scales" so they appear in the different sections.
- Staple pieces of feathers, fake fur, and scale-looking fabric in the corresponding sections.
- Enlarge the animals (p. 208). Duplicate several of each on white paper.
- Also enlarge and duplicate other animals that students may find interesting, including the lion (p. 168), fish (p. 153), monkey (p. 183), and owl (p. 189).
- Have students choose an animal and color it. Then have them glue a feather or a square of fur or a square of scale fabric to the animal to show its covering.
- Tell students to identify the animal and its covering before stapling it to the correct section of the bulletin board.

133 Face-to-Face with the Animals ✀✀

Science Standard ▶ Identifies the external characteristics of different kinds of animals that allow their needs to be met

- Prepare a bulletin board with the desired color of craft paper, a border, and the title "Face-to-Face with the Animals."
- Display resources about animals that have facial features that help them live in their environment, such as a rabbit with long ears and a frog that has big eyes on top of its head.
- Challenge students to choose an animal with such a characteristic and create its face on a large paper plate using construction paper and art supplies. Remind students to stress the feature that helps the animal.
- Then have students write a sentence on an index card that identifies the animal's special feature and its use.
- Staple the face and the card to the bulletin board in a pleasing arrangement.

Content-Related Bulletin Board Ideas

134 Amazing Animal Riddles

Language Arts Standard ▶ Writes in different forms for different purposes

- ▶ Prepare a bulletin board with the desired color of craft paper, a border, and the title "Amazing Animal Riddles."
- ▶ Enlarge the animal collage (p. 209) and trace it on white craft paper. Color it and cut it out. Staple it to the bulletin board.
- ▶ Have students fold a sheet of white construction paper in half. Challenge them to write a rhyming riddle about any animal in the collage on the top flap of the paper. Encourage students to include clues about the animal's special body features or characteristics. Then have students draw and color a picture of the animal on the inside of the paper.
- ▶ Staple the riddles to the bulletin board and encourage students to read and solve the riddles before lifting the flap to check their answer.

135 Perfect Pet Pals

Math Standard ▶ Constructs picture graphs

- ▶ Prepare a bulletin board with the desired color of craft paper, a border, and the title "Perfect Pet Pals." Draw the frame for a picture graph and write the kinds of pets on cards for the categories. Staple the cards along the left side of the graph.
- ▶ Cut white construction paper in half and provide one half for each student. Invite students to draw a horizontal picture of one pet they have on the construction paper. Suggest that students without pets draw a picture of the pet they would like to have.
- ▶ Have students staple their picture to the correct category on the picture graph.
- ▶ Ask questions that students can answer using the data on the graph.

136 Some "Bunny" Is Hiding!

Social Studies Standard ▶ Uses terms including *over, under, near, far, left,* and *right* to describe relative location

- ▶ Prepare a bulletin board with white craft paper.
- ▶ Create a forest scene with trees, water, rocks, flowers, and bushes.
- ▶ Add a border and the title "Some 'Bunny' Is Hiding!"
- ▶ Duplicate a rabbit (p. 208) on white paper for each student and cut the rabbits out. Ask students to color the rabbits.
- ▶ Invite students to tell where on the bulletin board they would hide if they were bunnies in the woods. Encourage students to use location words to describe the place.
- ▶ Staple the rabbits to the places that the students describe.

Bulletin Boards, SV 1-4190-1884-1

Environment

137 Lunch with the "Three *Rs*" ✂

Science Standard ▶ Identifies how to recycle, reduce, and reuse items at school

Materials

- lunch box pattern on page 210
- craft paper
- border
- scissors
- stapler
- glue
- pencils
- crayons or markers
- construction paper

Teacher Preparation

▶ Prepare a bulletin board with the desired color of craft paper, a border, and the title "Lunch with the 'Three Rs.'"

▶ Lead a discussion with students about how we all contribute to pollution and how we can help lower pollution by recycling, reusing, and reducing.

▶ Duplicate the lunch box (p. 210) for each student.

▶ When students have completed their lunch boxes, staple them on the bulletin board in a pleasing arrangement.

Note: Students may use the trash from their lunch box or from their lunch tray.

Student Directions

▶ Save the trash from a day's lunch. Exclude the food items.

▶ Color and cut out the picture of the lunch box.

▶ Glue the lunch box to a sheet of construction paper.

▶ Glue the trash items on the lunch box.

▶ Think about what you can do to help recycle, reuse, or reduce the trash in your lunch each day.

▶ Dictate or write a sentence below the picture of the lunch box telling about one thing you will do.

(page 25)

Additional Science Bulletin Board Ideas

138 Wanted: A Clean, Healthy Planet ✂✂

Science Standard ▶ Describes how to keep the environment clean

- ▶ Prepare a bulletin board with the desired color of craft paper, a border, and the title "Wanted: A Clean, Healthy Planet."
- ▶ Enlarge the Earth (p. 211). Then color it, cut it out, and staple it in the middle of the bulletin board.
- ▶ Lead a discussion with students about ways that people can stop air, land, water, and noise pollution.
- ▶ Provide students with markers and a half sheet of poster board. Have each student design a colorful poster that suggests a way to keep the environment clean. Challenge students to include a catchy slogan.
- ▶ Staple the posters on the bulletin board in a pleasing arrangement.

139 The Pollution Solution ✂✂✂

Science Standard ▶ Identifies how pollution harms the environment

- ▶ Prepare a bulletin board with the desired color of craft paper and the title "The Pollution Solution."
- ▶ Invite students to use paper plates, watercolor paints, and cotton balls to make the planet Earth. Have students paint the shapes of the continents and oceans on one side of a plate. Then have them pull apart the cotton balls and glue them on the plate to resemble clouds.
- ▶ Write a pollution situation like the ones listed below on the back of each paper plate.
  - Heera throws a plastic cup out of the car window.
  - Someone leaves an empty chips bag on the picnic table.
  - Maria throws some old batteries in the trash can.
  - Miss Mata pours house paint down the kitchen drain.
  - Mrs. Taylor puts the plastic milk jugs in the trash.
  - Mr. Kang empties his oil cans into the lake.
  - Sarah packs her lunch in plastic bags.
  - John's car has black smoke coming out of the exhaust pipe.
- ▶ Punch a hole through the edge of each plate and tie a three-inch piece of yarn through it.
- ▶ Staple the plates on the bulletin board in equal rows. Place the staple on the yarn so that the plates can be turned over to read the sentences on the back. Have the painted side of the plate displayed.
- ▶ Invite students to turn one Earth over and read the sentence on the back.
- ▶ Leave each plate turned over after it has been selected. Then have students write a sentence or paragraph telling how it harms the environment and a solution for the particular problem. Have them draw a picture of the solution.
- ▶ Staple students' work around the border of the bulletin board.

Content-Related Bulletin Board Ideas

140 Recycle These Letters into Words

Language Arts Standard ▶ Uses information learned to develop vocabulary

- Prepare a bulletin board with the desired color of craft paper, a border, and the title "Recycle These Letters into Words."
- Write the words *pollution, recycle, trash, ecology, reuse, litter, Earth,* and *garbage* on sentence strips. Cut the words apart and staple them in a column on the left side of the bulletin board.
- Enlarge the Earth (p. 211) and make eight copies. Color them and cut them out. Staple them on the bulletin board next to the column of words.
- Duplicate eight clouds (p. 226), cut them out, and number them. Scramble the words that are on the sentence strips and write the scrambled words on the clouds. Staple a cloud above each Earth.
- Have students read the vocabulary words and unscramble the words.

141 Reuse the Refuse

Math Standard ▶ Constructs picture graphs

- Prepare a bulletin board with the desired color of craft paper, a border, and the title "Reuse the Refuse." Use a yardstick to draw a graph on the craft paper that has three columns and seven rows.
- Write *Aluminum and Tin, Plastic and Glass,* and *Paper* at the bottom of each column.
- Duplicate the trash pictures (p. 212). Enlarge them to a size equal to the size of the cells on the grid. Color the pictures and cut them out.
- Invite students to use self-stick adhesive tape to place each picture of trash in the correct column of the graph.

142 Past, Present, Future

Social Studies Standard ▶ Identifies ways in which people have modified the physical environment

- Prepare a bulletin board with the desired color of craft paper, a border, and the title "Past, Present, Future."
- Enlarge the smog scene (p. 211) or trace it on the bulletin board.
- Lead a discussion with students about the scene and about how many things that make our lives easier add to the pollution of the air.
- Challenge students to draw a picture of what the scene might have looked like a hundred years ago. Have students research the types of homes and means of transportation that were common at that time and include them in their pictures. Staple their pictures on the bulletin board.
- Discuss what the scene might look like in the future if people continue to pollute the Earth.

nutrition

143 A Nutritious Meal ✄✄✄

Science Standard ▶ **Identifies types of nutrients**

Materials

- food pictures on page 213
- craft paper
- border
- paper plates
- scissors
- stapler
- glue
- pencils
- crayons or markers

Teacher Preparation

▶ Prepare a bulletin board with the desired color of craft paper, a border, and the title "A Nutritious Meal."

▶ Enlarge the chart below and staple it in the center of the bulletin board.

Nutrient	Food Source
Carbohydrate	Potato, bread, cereals, pasta
Protein	Fish, chicken, eggs, beans, peas
Fats	Oil, margarine, butter, nuts
Vitamin A	Carrots, apricots
Vitamin C	Tomatoes, oranges, strawberries
Calcium	Milk, cheese, yogurt
Iron	Spinach, liver

▶ Duplicate the bread slice, chicken, carrot, and yogurt (p. 213) for each student.

▶ Lead a discussion with students about the nutrients that their bodies need to stay healthy and about how they get them from various food sources.

▶ When students have completed their meal plates, staple the paper plates next to the chart on the bulletin board.

Student Directions

▶ Color and cut out the food.

▶ Glue them on the paper plate.

▶ Look at the chart. Then write the nutrient next to the food that provides it.

▶ Turn the plate over. Write the remaining nutrients that were not provided in this meal.

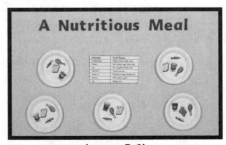

(page 26)

Additional Science Bulletin Board Ideas

144 Mission Nutrition ✂

Science Standard ▶ Identifies healthy and unhealthy food choices

- ▶ Prepare a bulletin board with the desired color of craft paper, a border, and the title "Mission Nutrition."
- ▶ Enlarge the lunch box (p. 210). Staple it in the middle of the bulletin board.
- ▶ Enlarge all of the food pictures (pp. 213 and 214). Color, laminate, and cut out the pictures.
- ▶ Lead a discussion with students about foods that are healthy for them and foods that are unhealthy.
- ▶ Explain that their mission is to find the healthy foods for their lunch.
- ▶ Invite students to use self-stick adhesive tape to place the healthy food pictures on the lunch box.
- ▶ Challenge students to tell why it is unhealthy to eat the other foods frequently.

145 Grouping the Foods on the Pyramid ✂✂

Science Standard ▶ Identifies food groups

- ▶ Prepare a bulletin board with the desired color of craft paper, a border, and the title "Grouping the Foods on the Pyramid."
- ▶ Enlarge the food pyramid (p. 215) onto the bulletin board.
- ▶ Color the climbing figure black and the sections of the pyramid from left to right orange, green, red, yellow, light blue, and purple.
- ▶ Cut off half the front side of a manila folder. Staple the sides together to form a pocket. Make six pockets.
- ▶ Color the short side of one pocket orange and label it *GRAINS*, color one green and label it *VEGETABLES*, color one red and label it *FRUITS*, color one yellow and label it *OILS*, color one light blue and label it *MILK*, and color one purple and label it *MEAT AND BEANS*. Staple the pockets below the pyramid.
- ▶ Enlarge the food pictures (pp. 213 and 214). Color and cut them out. Provide additional pictures from newspapers or magazines of foods in the oil group.
- ▶ Invite students to sort the food pictures by food groups. Have them put the pictures in the correct pocket.
- ▶ Challenge students to cut out additional food pictures from magazines and add them to the correct pockets.

Tip: Visit the web site www.mypyramid.gov for additional information on the current food pyramid.

Content-Related Bulletin Board Ideas

146 Going Graphic over Food

Math Standard ▶ **Uses organized data to construct bar-type graphs**

- ▶ Prepare a bulletin board with the desired color of craft paper, a border, and the title "Going Graphic over Food."
- ▶ Use a yardstick to make a graph in the middle of the bulletin board that has six rows and ten columns. Write the numbers *1–10* below each column.
- ▶ Enlarge 10 beans, 11 apples, 9 squash, 8 oranges, 7 heads of lettuce, and 6 bananas (p. 214). Color and cut them out.
- ▶ Staple one of each of the foods to the left of the six rows on the graph.
- ▶ Staple the remaining pictures of the beans together in a group near the graph. Repeat grouping the other foods together and stapling them near the graph.
- ▶ Cut 50 construction paper squares that are the same size as the cells on the graph.
- ▶ Invite students to count the grouped food items. Then have them use self-stick adhesive tape to place a paper square on the graph for each food, indicating how many there are of each.
- ▶ Discuss the completed graph. Ask students questions about the graph.

147 To the Market We Go

Social Studies Standard ▶ **Identifies the role of markets in the exchange of goods and services**

- ▶ Prepare a bulletin board with the desired color of craft paper, a border, and the title "To the Market We Go."
- ▶ Lead a discussion with students about how markets often provide goods that we need. Write *16¢, 28¢, 32¢, 35¢,* and *43¢* on the sides of five brown lunch bags.
- ▶ Select five food pictures (p. 213 and p. 214) and enlarge them. Color and cut them out. Glue one picture to the inside back of each bag so that it can easily be seen.
- ▶ Staple the opened bags with the money amount showing in a row across the middle of the bulletin board.
- ▶ Cut sentence strips in half so that there are five equal strips. Fold the strips in half lengthwise. Staple the ends of the strips together to form a pocket. Staple a pocket below each lunch bag.
- ▶ Duplicate ten pennies, five nickels, five dimes, and five quarters (p. 192). Color, laminate, and cut them out.
- ▶ Invite students to place the coins needed to buy each food item in the pocket below the bags.

Plants

148 "Seed" Us Grow! ✂✂

Science Standard ▶ **Identifies the parts of plants**

Materials

- flower patterns on page 216
- border
- blue, yellow, and brown craft paper
- students' school pictures
- students' baby pictures
- brown yarn

- a variety of colors of construction paper
- large craft sticks
- green crayons or markers
- glue
- scissors
- stapler

Teacher Preparation

▶ Cover the top two-thirds of the bulletin board with blue craft paper and the bottom third with brown craft paper.

▶ Cut out a sun from the yellow paper and staple it on the bulletin board.

▶ Add a border and the title "'Seed' Us Grow!"

▶ Make templates of the petal, leaf, center, and seed (p. 216).

▶ Staple students' completed flowers on the bulletin board.

Student Directions

▶ Color a craft stick green.

▶ Trace and cut out one yellow flower center. Glue it to one end of the stick.

▶ Trace and cut out one green seed. Glue it to the other end of the stick.

(page 26)

▶ Trace and cut out six petals in any color of paper. Glue them around the center.

▶ Trace and cut out two green leaves. Glue them to the stick.

▶ Glue your baby picture on the seed.

▶ Glue your school picture on the flower center.

▶ Cut pieces of yarn for roots. Glue them on the seed.

Additional Science Bulletin Board Ideas

149 How Does Your Garden Grow? ✂

Science Standard ▶ **Identifies plant needs**

- ▶ Cover the top two-thirds of the bulletin board with blue craft paper and the bottom third with brown craft paper. Add a border and the title "How Does Your Garden Grow?"
- ▶ Cut a generous supply of yellow tissue paper squares and foil squares.
- ▶ Cut three-inch circles of yellow, blue, white, and brown paper. Give one of each color to each student.
- ▶ Tell students that flowers need sun. Have them glue squares of yellow tissue paper to the yellow circle, representing the sun. Staple students' dried art in a circle, collage style, to form a sun in one corner of the bulletin board.
- ▶ Tell students that flowers need air. Have students glue cotton balls on the white circle, representing air. Staple them collage style to form a wind cloud. Draw lines to represent movement.
- ▶ Tell students that plants need water. Have students glue foil squares to the blue circle, representing water. Staple these circles to make individual raindrops on the opposite side of the bulletin board from the sun.
- ▶ For the soil that flowers need, have students spread glue on the brown circles and sprinkle soil over the glue. Staple these circles to the brown part of the bulletin board.
- ▶ Finally, have students make flowers by coloring a craft stick green and gluing a cupcake liner to one end. Staple the completed flowers to the bulletin board.

150 Plant Partners ✂✂✂

Science Standard ▶ **Identifies ways that living organisms depend on each other**

- ▶ Cover a bulletin board with white craft paper.
- ▶ Use brown and green craft paper to make trees. Use blue craft paper to make a lake. Paint or draw some flowers on the bulletin board.
- ▶ Add a border and the title "Plant Partners."
- ▶ Have partners research symbiotic relationships of plants. The relationships can be as simple as the food/fertilizing relationship between birds and flowers, or a more specific relationship, such as the acacia tree and ants.
- ▶ Have partners draw a picture to show the relationship and write a brief description. Allow them time to present their research to the class.
- ▶ Staple students' completed pictures and descriptions to the bulletin board.

Content-Related Bulletin Board Ideas

151 ▶ Branching Out with Words

Language Arts Standard Uses resources to find synonyms

- Cover a bulletin board with light blue craft paper. Add a border and the title "Branching Out with Words."
- Crush a piece of brown craft paper lengthwise. Spread it out slightly to make a tree trunk.
- Repeat the process with thinner pieces of brown craft paper to make six or seven branches.
- Enlarge the leaf (p. 216) to make a template. Trace and cut out a leaf from green paper for each tree branch.
- Write one word on each leaf that has several synonyms, such as *big* and *pretty*.
- Challenge students to write other words that are synonyms for the words you wrote on the leaves.
- Have students trace and cut out a green leaf, write a synonym on it, and tape the leaf to the correct tree branch.

152 ▶ A Handy Flower Garden

Math Standard ▶ Identifies, extends, and creates simple patterns

- Cover the top two-thirds of the bulletin board with blue craft paper and the bottom third with brown craft paper. Add a border and the title "A Handy Flower Garden."
- Enlarge the girl watering (p. 217) on white craft paper. Color and cut out the figure. Staple it on one side of the bulletin board.
- Next cut strips of green paper for flower stems.
- Choose three colors of paint and pour them in clean meat trays.
- To make flowers, dip your hand in a color of paint and make handprints on white paper. Allow them to dry, and then cut them out and glue a green stem to each.
- Create a color pattern on the bulletin board using the flowers.
- Invite students to choose a paint color from the meat trays and make a handprint on white paper. Allow their handprints to dry.
- Help students cut out the dried handprints and glue them as flowers on a stem. Help students continue the color pattern on the bulletin board with their flowers.

Rocks

153 Rocks Have Minerals

Science Standard ▶ Observes and describes differences in rocks

Materials

- rock pattern on page 218
- any color craft paper
- several colors of aquarium rocks
- bowls

- writing paper
- scissors
- stapler
- glue
- border

Teacher Preparation

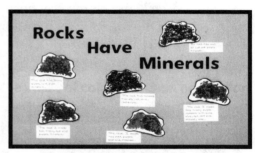

(page 27)

- ▶ Cover the bulletin board with craft paper.
- ▶ Add a border and the title "Rocks Have Minerals."
- ▶ Duplicate the rock (p. 218) for each student. Reduce or enlarge the pattern to the desired size.
- ▶ Fill each bowl with a different color of aquarium rocks.
- ▶ Lead a discussion with students about how rocks are made up of many different colored minerals. Compare the formation of rocks to that of baking a cake. Each type of cake is made from different ingredients just as each kind of rock is made of different minerals.
- ▶ After students have completed their work, staple their rocks and sentences in a pleasing arrangement on the bulletin board.

Student Directions

- ▶ Cut out the rock pattern.
- ▶ Use the different colored aquarium rocks as minerals. Glue the "minerals" on the rock pattern.
- ▶ Write a sentence on writing paper telling about the different colors of minerals on your rock. For example, if the rock has blue and red stones, you might write *My rock has blue and red minerals* or *The rock I made has blue and red minerals* or *This rock has minerals that are blue and red.*

Additional Science Bulletin Board Ideas

154   As Hard As a Rock   ✂

Science Standard ▶ Observes and describes properties of rocks

- Cover a bulletin board with the desired color of craft paper, a border, and the title "As Hard as a Rock." Draw a line down the middle of the bulletin board. On one side draw a picture of a rock and label that side *Hard Rocks*. On the other side draw a picture of a rock with a few minerals lying next to it and label that side *Soft Rocks*.
- Collect enough small rocks so that there is one for each student. Include some pieces of limestone or other soft rocks.
- Provide a small clay flower pot.
- Demonstrate to students how to determine if a rock is hard or soft by scratching the clay pot with the rock.
- If the rock is soft, the minerals will crumble off. If the rock is hard, the rock will scratch the clay pot.
- Duplicate the rock pattern (p. 218) for each student. Have them cut it out.
- Invite students to pick one rock from the collection and color their paper rock to match the rock.
- Then have students test their rock on the clay pot to see if it is hard or soft.
- Help students staple their rock drawings to the correct side of the bulletin board.

155   Getting to the Core of the Matter   ✂✂✂

Science Standard ▶ Identifies and records properties of soils

- Prepare a bulletin board with the desired color of craft paper, a border, and the title "Getting to the Core of the Matter."
- Discuss with students that scientists learn about the earth's core by drilling deep into it and extracting a sample of rocks. Explain that this core shows that the earth is made of layers of different kinds of rocks.
- Provide each student with an empty paper towel tube. Make available several types of craft items that can be glued on the tube such as fabric scraps, yarn, sand, glitter, cotton balls, and ribbon.
- Invite students to glue the craft items to cover their tube in layers from top to bottom, representing the rock layers in the earth's core.
- Staple the tubes to the bulletin board in a pleasing arrangement.

Content-Related Bulletin Board Ideas

156 Our Word Wall Rocks

Language Standard ▶ Spells high-frequency sight words correctly

- Prepare a bulletin board with brown craft paper covering the bottom two-thirds of the board. Cut the edge of the brown paper so that it has a rough look to it.
- Add a border and the title "Our Word Wall Rocks."
- Duplicate several copies of the rock (p. 218) for each student. Have them color the rocks gray and cut them out.
- Have students write a familiar high-frequency word on each rock.
- Help students staple their rocks close together on the bulletin board to resemble a rock wall.

157 Let's Rock Around the Clock

Math Standard ▶ Tells time to the hour and half-hour

- Prepare a bulletin board with the desired color of craft paper, a border, and the title "Let's Rock Around the Clock."
- Duplicate several copies of the clock face (p. 207). Draw hands on each clock to represent different hours and half hours. Staple the clocks on the bulletin board in a pleasing arrangement.
- Duplicate a rock (p. 218) for each clock. Color each rock and cut it out.
- Cut sentence strips the width of the clocks. Fold each piece lengthwise. Staple the ends of the strips to the bulletin board to form a pocket below each clock.
- Write the times designated on each clock on the rocks.
- Challenge students to place the rocks in the correct pocket below each clock.

Classroom Management

158 We "Lava" Good Listeners

- Cover a bulletin board with white craft paper.
- Use the volcano (p. 219) as a guide to draw a volcano on the bulletin board.
- Add a border and the title "We 'Lava' Good Listeners."
- Provide each student with a rock (p. 218). Have them cut out the rocks and color them to resemble "hot lava."
- Have students write their name on the lava rock. Staple their rock on the volcano when they demonstrate good listening skills.

Safety

159 Safety Is the Goal! ✂✂

Science Standard ▶ **Identifies safety rules during play**

Materials

- light blue and gray craft paper
- border
- yellow crepe paper
- large paper plates
- crayons or markers
- newspaper
- pencils
- clear tape
- scissors
- stapler

Teacher Preparation

▶ Prepare a bulletin board with the light blue craft paper, a border, and the title "Safety Is the Goal!"

▶ Cut three two-foot long strips of the gray craft paper. Roll them to make tubes for the frame of a soccer goal. Staple two of tubes on the bulletin board parallel to make the upright bars of the goal. Staple the third tube perpendicular to the uprights to make the top crosspiece.

▶ Cut the crepe paper into streamers that are the same length as the gray tubes.

▶ Tape streamers to the top bar of the goal frame so they are six inches apart. Allow them to hang straight down.

▶ Tape more streamers to the left bar so they are six inches apart.

▶ Weave the streamers to make a net. Tape the ends to the right bar.

▶ Allow students to share the rules on their soccer balls before stapling the completed soccer balls to the bulletin board.

Student Directions

▶ Draw and color a geometric pattern on the back of a paper plate to make a soccer ball.

▶ Write a rule on the ball that tells a safe practice for any kind of physical activity, including a sport activity or playground participation.

(page 27)

▶ Place the soccer ball plate on top of another white paper plate so that the backs face out.

▶ Crumple a large sheet of newspaper.

▶ Place the crumpled paper between the two plates. Staple around the edges of the plates to seal them.

Additional Science Bulletin Board Ideas

160 Have a Ball, But Stay Safe! ✂

Science Standard ▶ Follows rules, procedures, and safe practices

▶ Prepare a bulletin board with the desired color of craft paper, a border, and the title "Have a Ball, But Stay Safe!"

▶ Display a variety of balls, including rubber, tennis, baseball, soccer, and golf.

▶ Discuss with students some rules to follow when playing with the different balls. Stress the most important rule—people must maintain a safe distance from others when playing with balls.

▶ Invite students to make their favorite ball. Give each student a white bag. Have them crumple newspaper to put inside. Help them form a sphere and tape it closed. Tell them to paint their ball.

▶ Invite students to share the balls they made.

▶ Have students identify places you can staple the balls on the bulletin board. Stress that students remember to keep a safe distance between balls as if they were playing. As the bulletin board gets crowded, help students find a place that is not close to other balls.

161 "Bee" Safe—Use the Right Equipment ✂✂✂

Science Standard ▶ Selects and uses the appropriate safety equipment

▶ Prepare a bulletin board with the desired color of craft paper, a border, and the title "'Bee' Safe—Use the Right Equipment."

▶ Enlarge a bee (p. 206) and trace it on yellow craft paper. Color the stripes black and cut out the bee. Staple it to the bulletin board.

▶ Invite students to draw a picture of themselves dressed in the gear of a favorite sport. Tell them to include all the protective equipment. Then have them label the equipment to make a diagram.

▶ Have students write a sentence for each labeled part that tells how the equipment keeps them safe.

▶ Staple students' completed drawings and sentences on the bulletin board.

Content-Related Bulletin Board Ideas

162 HELP! Call 911!

Math Standard ▶ Reads numbers to 10

- ▶ Prepare a bulletin board with the desired color of craft paper, a border, and the title "HELP! Call 911!"
- ▶ Enlarge the telephone (p. 220) and trace it on gray craft paper.
- ▶ Cut foam into nine squares to make the telephone buttons and write the numbers *1–9* on them. Glue the foam squares on the telephone.
- ▶ Duplicate a telephone information page (p. 221) for each student.
- ▶ Discuss with students what qualifies as an emergency. Then tell students about the emergency phone number 911.
- ▶ Invite each student to "push" the telephone buttons to show the number they can call if someone is hurt.
- ▶ Then tell them the information they need to give, including their name, address, and phone number.
- ▶ Have students write or dictate their own information on the telephone information page.
- ▶ Staple the telephones to the bulletin board after students practice "dialing" 911 again.

163 Safe in the Community

Social Studies Standard ▶ Identifies the importance of jobs

- ▶ Prepare a bulletin board with the desired color of craft paper, a border, and the title "Safe in the Community."
- ▶ Enlarge the safe (p. 222) and trace it on gray craft paper. Cut out the figure, color the features, and staple it to the bulletin board.
- ▶ Duplicate a paper doll (p. 248) for each student.
- ▶ Discuss with students the different jobs in the community that keep people safe. Encourage creative brainstorming, especially for older students, to include such workers as doctors, sanitation specialists, teachers, and store clerks (who keep dangerous materials in locked cabinets).
- ▶ Challenge students to color a paper doll to represent someone who keeps the community safe. Have them cut out the figure.
- ▶ Have students cut out a speech bubble. Tell students to write sentences on the speech bubble to identify the job their person has and what the person does to keep the community safe.
- ▶ Staple students' completed work on the bulletin board.

Solar System

164 ▷ Where Is the Sun? ✂

Science Standard ▶ Observes, describes, and records changes in position

Materials

blue craft paper, border, large paper plates, yellow tissue paper, liquid starch, clean meat tray, magazines, large resealable bags, self-stick adhesive tape, pencils, scissors, stapler

Teacher Preparation

▶ Prepare a bulletin board with blue craft paper, a border, and the title "Where Is the Sun?"

▶ Cut the yellow tissue paper into one-inch squares.

▶ Pour a small amount of liquid starch into the meat tray.

▶ Cut out several pictures showing different activities that students do, such as sleeping, eating lunch, and playing outdoors.

▶ Draw an arc across the bulletin board from the bottom left corner to the bottom right corner to show the path of the sun. Place tape in each corner, at the apex of the circle, and two equally spaced between the corner and the apex.

▶ Staple the back of a resealable bag on the bulletin board so that it is directly under the apex of the circle. Place the pictures in the unsealed bag.

▶ Discuss how the sun moves across the sky and show its position in the early morning, midmorning, noon, afternoon, evening, and night.

▶ Show students the different magazine pictures and have them identify the activities. Ask them to tell the sun's position for each picture. Put the sun on the tape in the correct places.

▶ During free time, allow partners to choose pictures of activities and put the sun in the correct place for each activity.

Student Directions

▶ Work with the other students to make a sun. Dip a square of tissue paper in the starch and put it on the back of the plate. Overlap the edges. Cover the plate to make the sun.

▶ Cut out pictures from magazines of people doing different activities.

▶ Think of where the sun's position is when people do those activities. Put the sun in that place.

(page 28)

Bulletin Boards, SV 1-4190-1884-1

Additional Science Bulletin Board Ideas

165 Star Light, Star Bright Patterns ✂✂

Science Standard ▶ **Knows that organisms, objects, and events have properties and patterns**

- Prepare a bulletin board with black craft paper, a border, and the title "Star Light, Star Bright Patterns."
- Explain what constellations are, and have students do research to find information about different constellations.
- Have them choose one constellation to duplicate on black paper. Have them use a pencil to punch holes in black paper to show the pattern.
- Give students yellow chalk to write the name of the constellation under the punched pattern.
- Have students glue a yellow sheet of paper behind the black paper so the "stars" shine through. Invite students to share their constellations and the interesting details they learned.

166 A Group "Plan-et" Project ✂✂✂

Science Standard ▶ **Identifies the planets in the solar system and their position in relation to the Sun**

- Prepare the bulletin board with black craft paper, a border, and the title "A Group 'Plan-et' Project."
- Trace a sun (p. 225) on yellow craft paper and cut it out. Staple it to the left edge of the bulletin board.
- Duplicate a set of planets (p. 223) for each student. Challenge each student to make a diagram of the planet order. Have students color, cut out, and glue the planets in order from the sun on a sheet of paper.
- Next assign students to work in one of nine groups, one group for each planet. Tell students they will work cooperatively to plan the bulletin board. Provide additional resources and tell students to find facts about their planet.
- Challenge students to use this information and their diagrams to determine the size relationship of their planet to the sun on the bulletin board. Encourage them to make a replica of their planet using paper bags, construction paper, and other art supplies.
- Have students write facts about their planet on index cards that they staple to a piece of yarn and hang from their planet.
- Have students staple the completed planets in the correct order on the bulletin board.

Content-Related Bulletin Board Ideas

167 Blasting Off to the Stars

Language Arts Standard ▶ Knows the order of the alphabet

- ▶ Prepare a bulletin board with dark blue craft paper and the title "Blasting Off to the Stars."
- ▶ Trace 26 stars (p. 224) on yellow paper and cut them out. Write a letter of the alphabet on each. Staple the stars to the bulletin board so they are not in alphabetical order.
- ▶ Next duplicate a nose cone (p. 225) and two fins (p. 224) on white paper for each student. Tell students to color and cut out the figures in order to make a rocket.
- ▶ Have students decorate a paper towel tube with art supplies. Then, help them wrap the nose cone around one end of the tube and glue it in place. Have students fold the fins on the dotted lines and glue them to the bottom of the tube.
- ▶ You may wish to have students cut 12-inch crepe streamers to glue to the bottom of the paper towel tube.
- ▶ Challenge students to use their rockets to visit the stars in alphabetical order. Allow each student the opportunity to do so.
- ▶ Staple the completed rockets to the bulletin board to make a border.

168 A Real Night Light

Math Standard ▶ Uses a calendar

- ▶ Prepare a bulletin board with dark blue craft paper, a border, and the title "A Real Night Light."
- ▶ Use yellow paint to make a calendar that covers the bulletin board.
- ▶ Write the name of the month and the days of the week on yellow cards and staple them on the calendar.
- ▶ Paint the numerals to show the dates for the month.
- ▶ Cut out three-inch circles, one for each night of the month.
- ▶ Lead students in a discussion of the moon and its phases. Adjust the description and vocabulary to fit the level of the students.
- ▶ Invite students to be moon watchers for the month to see how it changes each night.
- ▶ Write the name of a student on the calendar to assign the night the student will watch the moon. Each day, have a different moon watcher report on the moon's shape. Help the student cut the three-inch circle to make a replica of the moon's shape. If the moon was not visible, discuss whether weather caused the invisibility or if the moon was in the phase where it could not be seen.
- ▶ Staple each student's completed moon to the calendar.

Weather

169 Name That Cloud ✂✂

Science Standard ▶ **Observes and names three common cloud formations**

Materials

- cloud patterns on page 226
- blue craft paper
- drawing paper
- stapler
- sentence strips
- crayons or markers

Teacher Preparation

▶ Cover the bulletin board with blue craft paper and add the title "Name That Cloud."

▶ Duplicate one or two clouds (p. 226) for each student.

▶ Have students cut out the clouds and staple the clouds around the bulletin board for the border.

▶ Write the name of each cloud on a sentence strip: *Cumulus Clouds*, *Cirrus Clouds*, *Stratus Clouds*. Staple the sentence strips below the bulletin board title.

▶ Write the following facts about each cloud on sentence strips. Staple them below the name of each cloud.

- *Cumulus Clouds:* They are puffy and white. They are low in the sky and are flat across the bottom. They usually mean fair, warm weather.
- *Cirrus Clouds:* They are white and feathery. They are the highest clouds. They usually mean cool or cold weather.
- *Stratus Clouds:* They look like a low gray blanket. They bring rain or snow. They bring fog when at ground level.

▶ Divide students into three groups. Assign one cloud type to each group.

▶ Help students staple their pictures below the description of their assigned cloud.

Student Directions

▶ Cut out one or two clouds to be used for the border.

▶ Read the description of the cloud for the group.

▶ Draw a picture on drawing paper of the kind of clothes that would be worn during this kind of weather.

(page 28)

Additional Science Bulletin Board Ideas

170 Weather Watch ✂

Science Standard ▶ Observes and records weather changes

- Cover a bulletin board with white craft paper and add a border and the title "Weather Watch."
- Draw a calendar grid with five rows and seven columns. Write the days of the week at the top of each column.
- During one month, have students check the weather forecast each morning, using either the newspaper, radio, or Internet.
- Ask volunteers to draw a picture on the correct date of the calendar, indicating what the weather is.
- You may wish to have students take turns observing the weather on days that there is no school. Have them record it on the calendar when they return.
- At the end of the month, lead a discussion with students about the types of weather observed.

171 The Ups and Downs of the Water Cycle ✂✂✂

Science Standard ▶ Describes the water cycle

- Cover the bulletin board with craft paper. Add a border and the title "The Ups and Downs of the Water Cycle."
- Use the water cycle chart (p. 227) as a guide to prepare a bulletin board. Enlarge and trace the chart or draw it on the bulletin board.
- Lead a discussion with students about how water changes its form in the water cycle. Explain to them about evaporation, precipitation, and condensation, which are the three main steps in the water cycle.
- Duplicate the raindrop (p. 226) for each student.
- Assign each student to write a description of one of the three main steps in the water cycle. Have them write the description on their raindrop.
- Next have students color and cut out the raindrop.
- Help students staple their raindrop on the correct section of the bulletin board.

Content-Related Bulletin Board Ideas

172 Dropping In on Blends

Language Standard ▶ Knows beginning blends

- Prepare a bulletin board with blue craft paper. Add a border and the title "Dropping In on Blends."
- Enlarge the cloud (p. 226) and make three clouds. Write a target beginning blend on each cloud. Staple them next to each other on the bulletin board.
- Duplicate several raindrops (p. 226) per cloud on blue construction paper. Cut them out.
- On each raindrop, glue a picture from a magazine or draw a picture of an object whose name begins with one of the target blends.
- Invite students to use self-stick adhesive tape to match the raindrops with the correct target blend.

173 A Shower of Shapes

Math Standard ▶ Identifies basic shapes

- Prepare a bulletin board with blue craft paper. Add a border and the title "A Shower of Shapes."
- Enlarge, color, and cut out an umbrella (p. 227) and six raindrops (p. 226).
- Draw a circle, a square, a triangle, a rectangle, an oval, and a diamond on each raindrop. Make a second matching set of raindrops. Place self-stick adhesive tape on the back of the second set of raindrops.
- Staple the umbrella in the center of the bulletin board. Staple one set of raindrops around the umbrella.
- Have students take turns matching the second set of raindrops to the correct raindrops on the bulletin board. Have them name each shape as they match it.

174 The Sky's the Limit

Social Studies Standard ▶ Identifies jobs in the community

- Prepare a bulletin board with blue craft paper. Add a border and the title "The Sky's the Limit."
- Duplicate the cloud (p. 226) for each student. Enlarge the clouds, if desired.
- Lead a discussion with students about various jobs that people do.
- Invite students to write a sentence on their cloud telling what job they want to do when they grow up.
- Staple the clouds in a pleasing arrangement on the bulletin board.

Character Education

175 All Kinds of Kindness ✂

Social Studies Standard ▸ **Identifies characteristics of good citizenship**

Materials

- tree pattern on page 228
- apple patterns on page 229
- craft paper
- border
- red, brown, green, and white construction paper
- old file folders

- scissors
- stapler
- glue
- pencils
- crayons or markers
- overhead projector

Teacher Preparation

▸ Prepare a bulletin board with the desired color of craft paper and the title "All Kinds of Kindness."

▸ Enlarge the tree (p. 228). Color and cut it out.

▸ Staple the tree in the middle of the bulletin board.

▸ Duplicate several apples, stems, and leaves (p. 229) for each student.

▸ Enlarge the same apple, stem, and leaf and trace them on the folders to use as templates. Cut them out.

▸ Discuss with students how the apple can be a symbol of caring and kindness.

▸ When students have completed their small apples, help them staple their apples along the border in a pattern.

▸ Staple students' completed large apples to the tree. If the tree is full, staple the remaining apples next to the tree.

Student Directions

▸ Color and cut out several red, yellow, and green apples. Color and cut out the stems and leaves. Glue them on the apples.

▸ Use the templates to trace an apple on red construction paper, a stem on brown construction paper, and a leaf on green construction paper. Cut them all out. Glue the parts of the apple together.

(page 29)

▸ Write or dictate a sentence on this apple telling one thing you can do to show kindness.

Additional Social Studies Bulletin Board Ideas

176 Being Responsible Is "Tree-mendous" ✂✂

Social Studies Standard ▶ **Identifies characteristics of good citizenship such as responsibility**

- Prepare a bulletin board with the desired color of craft paper, a border, and the title "Being Responsible Is 'Tree-mendous.'"
- Enlarge the tree (p. 228). Then color it, cut it out, and staple it on the left side of the bulletin board.
- Write the heading *I am responsible when I . . .* next to the tree. Underneath this heading write each of the following on a separate line: *complete my work assignment, keep my desk neat, throw away trash at lunch, come to class on time,* and *turn in my homework.*
- Discuss with students the meaning of responsibility. Explain to them that there are consequences when people ignore or fail to meet their responsibilities.
- Have students read the list of responsibilities on the bulletin board.
- Duplicate a generous supply of leaves (p. 229). Have students help cut them out.
- Staple the sides of a file folder together to form a pocket. Place the supply of leaves in the pocket and staple it in the corner of the bulletin board.
- Invite students to write their name and what they did on a leaf each time they complete a task on the list.
- Help students staple their leaves on or around the tree.

177 Good Citizens of Long Ago ✂✂✂

Social Studies Standard ▶ **Identifies historical figures who have exemplified good citizenship**

- Prepare a bulletin board with the desired color of craft paper, a border, and the title "Good Citizens of Long Ago."
- Duplicate a tree (p. 228) for each student. Have them color and cut it out.
- Then have them use that tree as a template and trace around it on white construction paper. Have students cut the tree out so that it matches the first tree.
- Place the colored tree on top of the white tree and staple them together across the top.
- Lead a discussion with students about the meaning of good citizenship. Then invite them to research a historical figure who exemplified good citizenship, such as John Chapman, Helen Keller, or Harriet Tubman.
- Challenge students to write a clue on the colored tree about what that person did that showed good citizenship. Have them lift the colored tree and write the name of and draw a picture of their historical figure on the white tree.
- Staple students' completed trees on the bulletin board in a pleasing arrangement.

Content-Related Bulletin Board Ideas

178 What's the Rule?

Math Standard ▶ Identifies and extends patterns to make predictions and solve problems

- ▶ Prepare a bulletin board with the desired color of craft paper, a border, and the title "What's the Rule?"
- ▶ Duplicate the apple, stem, and leaf (p. 229) for each student. Have students color and cut them out. Then have students glue the stem and leaf on the apple.
- ▶ Staple students' completed apples on the bulletin board in four equal rows. Write number patterns on the apples, such as *25, 27, 29, 31* (Rule: add two) or *44, 41, 38, 35* (Rule: take away three). Leave the last two apples in each row blank.
- ▶ Invite students to look at each row of apples for a pattern. Then have students write on a sheet of paper two more numbers to complete each pattern. Finally, have them write the rule.
- ▶ Staple students' papers around the apples on the bulletin board.

179 The Seasons of the Apple Tree

Science Standard ▶ Observes and describes parts of plants

- ▶ Prepare a bulletin board with the desired color of craft paper, a border, and the title "The Seasons of the Apple Tree."
- ▶ Discuss with students how trees change during the seasons.
- ▶ Invite each student to fold a large sheet of paper into fourths. Have students label each section *Winter, Spring, Summer,* and *Fall.*
- ▶ Have students draw a brown tree trunk with branches in each of the four sections of the paper. Have them draw snow with chalk for the winter tree. Have students draw green leaves on the second trunk and glue pink tissue paper squares on the tree for blossoms for the spring tree. For the summer tree, have students dip the eraser end of a pencil in green paint and stamp circles on the tree for the green apples. Finally, have students put red sticker dots on the fall tree for the red apples.
- ▶ Staple the pictures on the bulletin board in a pleasing arrangement.

Communities

180　Open the Door to the Past ✂✂✂

Social Studies Standard ▶ **Understands common characteristics of communities, past and present**

Materials

door pattern on page 230, craft paper, border, small pizza boxes (one per student), construction paper, drawing paper, tape, scissors, stapler, glue, pencils, crayons or markers, overhead projector

Teacher Preparation

▶ Prepare a bulletin board with the desired color of craft paper, a border, and the title "Open the Door to the Past."

▶ Enlarge the door (p. 230). Color and cut it out.

▶ Staple the door in the middle of the bulletin board.

▶ Tape the corners of the pizza boxes so that boxes will not flatten when the lid is raised.

▶ Discuss with students the needs that a community in the present has in common with a community in the past. Examples of things needed by both communities are law enforcement, education, transportation, medical services, food, clothing, and shelter.

▶ When students have completed their "doors," open the lids and staple them to the bulletin board through the bottom of the box. Then close the lids on the boxes.

▶ Have students open the "doors" and read the descriptions.

Student Directions

▶ Decorate the lid of a pizza box to resemble a door with a window and a doorknob.

▶ Research a need that is common to communities in the past and the present.

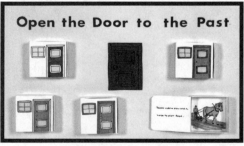

(page 29)

▶ Cut a sheet of drawing paper to fit the inside bottom of the box. Draw a picture on it that illustrates how a community in the past met that need. Glue the picture in the bottom of the pizza box.

▶ Write or dictate a sentence on a separate sheet of paper, describing your picture. Glue the description on the inside of the lid.

Bulletin Boards, SV 1-4190-1884-1

Additional Social Studies Bulletin Board Ideas

181 People in Our School Community ✂

Social Studies Standard ▶ **Identifies the responsibilities of authority figures in the school community**

- ▶ Prepare a bulletin board with black craft paper, a border, and the title "People in Our School Community."
- ▶ Take students on a tour of the school and introduce them to authority figures such as the principal, the counselor, the librarian, and the nurse. Discuss with students the responsibilities of each person.
- ▶ Duplicate the photo frame (p. 231) for each student. Invite them to cut out the photo frame and draw a picture on it of one of the authority figures in the school.
- ▶ Then have students write or dictate a sentence telling about one of the responsibilities of the authority figure on a separate sheet of paper.
- ▶ Staple the sentences below the photos in an arrangement that resembles an old-fashioned scrapbook.

182 Picture Perfect Communities ✂✂

Social Studies Standard ▶ **Describes similarities and differences in ways families meet basic human needs**

- ▶ Prepare a bulletin board with the desired color of craft paper, a border, and the title "Picture Perfect Communities."
- ▶ Enlarge and color the man with the camera (p. 232) and staple it on the right side of the bulletin board.
- ▶ Write the words *Rural, Suburban,* and *Urban* on sentence strips. Staple the three words side by side below the title.
- ▶ Lead a discussion with students about rural, suburban, and urban communities. Explain that rural communities are centered around small towns, suburban communities are near big cities, and urban communities are in large cities. Tell students that each type of community meets the needs of the people who live there.
- ▶ Assign students to research a rural, a suburban, or an urban community.
- ▶ Provide students with a large sheet of white construction paper. Have them accordion fold it in quarters.
- ▶ Invite students to make a travel brochure about the community they researched. First have them name the community. Then have them describe and illustrate the types of transportation, stores, restaurants, recreation facilities, and schools that are available in their community.
- ▶ Have students tell why their community would be a nice place to live or visit.
- ▶ Help students staple their brochures below the correct community label.

Content-Related Bulletin Board Ideas

183 Addresses Are Important

Language Arts Standard ▶ Writes in different forms for different purposes

- Prepare a bulletin board with the desired color of craft paper, a border, and the title "Addresses Are Important."
- Enlarge and color the mailbox (p. 233). Cut it out and staple it in the middle of the bulletin board.
- Use scissors to fringe strips of green construction paper to make grass. Staple the strips along the bottom of the bulletin board.
- Discuss with students that homes and businesses have addresses to help people locate them.
- Provide students with a local telephone book and two blank envelopes.
- Have them address one envelope to themselves by writing their name and home address. Then have students find the name of a familiar business in the phone book and address the second envelope to that business. You may wish to have older students locate the business on a map.
- Staple students' envelopes on the bulletin board next to the mailbox in a pleasing arrangement.

184 Picture This

Math Standard ▶ Orders numbers to 10

- Prepare a bulletin board with the desired color of craft paper, a border, and the title "Picture This."
- Enlarge and cut out ten photo frames (p. 231).
- Select ten pictures of community helpers and their tools (p. 234 and p. 235). Duplicate one copy of the first picture, two copies of the second, and so on. Continue until there are ten copies of the tenth picture. Cut out the pictures and glue them in the frames in sets from one to ten. It may be necessary to reduce the pictures for the larger sets in order to fit each set on one frame.
- Staple the sides of a manila folder together to form a pocket. Place the ten frames inside the pocket and staple it in the middle of the bulletin board.
- Cut sentence strips in ten lengths slightly longer than the width of the frames. Fold the strips lengthwise and staple the ends together to form pockets. Write a number from 1–10 on each pocket. Staple these pockets in a row across the bottom of the bulletin board.
- Invite students to count the items on each frame and place the frame in the pocket with the correct number.

Economics

185 The Story of a Store ✂✂✂

Social Studies Standard ▶ **Gives examples of how a simple business operates**

Materials

- store pattern on page 236
- craft paper
- border
- empty shoe boxes
- construction paper
- scissors
- stapler
- glue
- pencils
- crayons or markers
- overhead projector
- writing paper

Teacher Preparation

▶ Prepare a bulletin board with the desired color of craft paper, a border, and the title "The Story of a Store."

▶ Enlarge and color the store (p. 236) in the middle of the bulletin board.

▶ Discuss with students how a simple business operates.

▶ Provide students with empty shoe boxes, construction paper, and glue.

▶ When students have completed their "stores," remove the storefront lid from the boxes. Place the bottoms of the shoe boxes against the bulletin board and staple them to the bulletin board in a pleasing arrangement. Then replace the lid on the shoe box.

▶ Staple students' paragraphs below their stores.

Student Directions

▶ Cover a shoe box and the lid with construction paper.

▶ Decide what kind of store or business you want to make.

▶ Decorate the lid of the shoe box to resemble a storefront. Include windows, a door, and the name of the store.

▶ Write a paragraph on a sheet of paper about the store and how it operates.

(page 30)

Bulletin Boards, SV 1-4190-1884-1

Additional Social Studies Bulletin Board Ideas

186 It's Off to Work We Go! ✂

Social Studies Standard ▶ Understands the importance of jobs

- ▶ Prepare a bulletin board with the desired color of craft paper and the title "It's Off to Work We Go!"
- ▶ Enlarge the community helpers (p. 234 and p. 235).
- ▶ Provide students with a copy of each helper. Have students color and cut them out.
- ▶ Staple the community helpers around the edge of the bulletin board to make a border.
- ▶ Discuss with students the jobs they would like to do when they grow up and why they would like to do those jobs.
- ▶ Invite students to draw a picture of themselves doing a job that might interest them someday. Then have them write or dictate a sentence that tells what they like about that job.
- ▶ Staple students' completed pictures and sentences on the bulletin board in a pleasing arrangement.

187 Serve Up the Goods ✂✂

Social Studies Standard ▶ Identifies ways people exchange goods and services

- ▶ Prepare a bulletin board with the desired color of craft paper, a border, and the title "Serve Up the Goods."
- ▶ Discuss with students how some people provide goods in the community and some people provide services. Explain that each job requires certain equipment and sometimes a particular uniform.
- ▶ Enlarge the community helper cards (p. 234 and p. 235). Color them and cut them out.
- ▶ Staple the eight pictures of the helpers in two rows in the middle of the bulletin board. Leave space between the rows.
- ▶ Cut sentence strips into eight pieces the same width as the picture cards. Fold each piece lengthwise and staple the ends together to form pockets. Staple a pocket below each community helper.
- ▶ Invite students to place a picture of an object that is related to each person's job in the pocket below that person.
- ▶ Then have students write a paragraph telling about a time when they used a service of one of the helpers. Have students illustrate their paragraph.
- ▶ Staple students' completed pictures and paragraphs on the bulletin board in a pleasing arrangement.

Content-Related Bulletin Board Ideas

188 Help the Helpers

Language Arts Standard ▶ Uses nouns and verbs in sentences

- ▶ Prepare a bulletin board with the desired color of craft paper, a border, and the title "Help the Helpers."
- ▶ Enlarge the plumber, mail carrier, mechanic, firefighter, police officer, and doctor (p. 234 and p. 235) on white paper. Color and cut them out.
- ▶ Place a small ball of poster putty on the back of each cutout.
- ▶ Write simple sentences on sentence strips describing the jobs these people do, leaving out the nouns. Sentences might include *The _____ takes your temperature* or *The _____ puts out fires.* Leave a space wide enough for the cutouts to fit in the blank spaces. Staple the sentence strips to the bulletin board in a pleasing design.
- ▶ Make a pocket by cutting a sentence strip the width of the people and folding it lengthwise. Staple each end to the bulletin board. Put the cutouts in the pocket.
- ▶ Invite students to attach the cutouts to the correct sentences and read the sentences aloud.

189 Go to Great Lengths

Math Standard ▶ Measures length using standard units

- ▶ Prepare a bulletin board with the desired color of craft paper, a border, and the title "Go to Great Lengths."
- ▶ Enlarge and color the carpenter (p. 176) on the right side of the bulletin board.
- ▶ Draw three different lengths of lumber on the remaining section of the bulletin board using the board (p. 176) as a guide. Set the lumber one on top of the other.
- ▶ Provide students with a tape measure. Then invite each student to use it to measure the lengths of the three boards. Have students write the lengths on a sheet of paper.
- ▶ Staple students' papers on the bulletin board.

Classroom Management

190 We're Patrolling for Good Workers

- ▶ Prepare a bulletin board with the desired color of craft paper, a border, and the title "We're Patrolling for Good Workers."
- ▶ Enlarge and color the police officer (p. 234) in the middle of the bulletin board.
- ▶ Duplicate a star (p. 224) on yellow construction paper for each student. Have students cut it out and write their name on it.
- ▶ Have students select a work sample of which they are proud.
- ▶ Staple their work on the bulletin board in a pleasing design. Then staple the star with their name on it on the corner of their work.

Bulletin Boards, SV 1-4190-1884-1

Government

Be Wise—Follow These School Rules ✂

Social Studies Standard ▶ **Identifies rules that provide order, security, and safety**

Materials

- owl pattern on page 237
- owl parts patterns on page 238
- craft paper
- border
- brown paper bags
- yellow, brown, and white construction paper
- brown feathers
- black crayon
- pencils
- white copy paper
- scissors
- glue
- stapler

Teacher Preparation

▶ Prepare a bulletin board with the desired color of craft paper and a border.

▶ Duplicate an owl (p. 237) on brown paper. Cut it out.

▶ Trace and cut out a beak from yellow paper that is the same as the one on the owl pattern. Glue it on the owl. Trace and cut out two eyes from white paper that are the same as the ones on the owl pattern. Glue them on the owl. Staple the completed owl on the bulletin board.

▶ Add the title "Be Wise—Follow These School Rules." Use the owl's eyes for the two *o*'s in *School*.

▶ Trace a beak (p. 238) on yellow paper for each student. Cut them out.

▶ Trace two eyes (p. 238) on white paper for each student. Cut them out.

▶ Trace a tuft (p. 238) and two wings (p. 238) on brown paper for each student. Cut them out.

▶ Cut a speech bubble out of the copy paper for each student.

▶ Lead students in a discussion of why schools have rules. Help students brainstorm some important school rules.

▶ Staple students' completed owl puppets and speech bubbles to the bulletin board.

(page 30)

Student Directions

▶ Use a black crayon to make large pupils on two white eyes. Glue the eyes to a brown paper bag to make an owl puppet.

▶ Glue a beak and tuft, two wings, and some feathers on the owl puppet.

▶ Think of an important school rule. Write or dictate it on a speech bubble.

Additional Social Studies Bulletin Board Ideas

192 Our Eyes Are on the Leaders ✂✂

Social Studies Standard ▶ Compares roles of public officials

- ▶ Prepare a bulletin board with black craft paper.
- ▶ Use crepe paper streamers to divide the bulletin board into thirds.
- ▶ Add a border and the title "Our Eyes Are on the Leaders."
- ▶ Enlarge the town (p. 240) and the United States map (p. 241) and trace them on white craft paper. Color and cut them out
- ▶ Trace an enlarged outline of your state using the United States map.
- ▶ Staple the town on the left side of the bulletin board, the state outline in the center, and the United States map on the right side.
- ▶ Make four pockets by cutting sentence strips and folding them lengthwise. Staple one pocket under each picture and the fourth pocket in a lower corner of the bulletin board.
- ▶ Write *mayor, governor,* and *President* on the corresponding pockets under the town, state, and U.S. maps.
- ▶ Find and cut out pictures of your town's mayor, state's governor, and the President. Laminate the pictures and put them in the corner pocket.
- ▶ Invite each student to make a pair of eyes using art supplies. Staple the completed eyes to the bulletin board.
- ▶ Discuss the jobs of the different leaders and their names.
- ▶ Invite students to identify the people in the pictures and match them to the place they serve as leader.

193 Whooo Are the Leaders in This Town? ✂✂✂

Social Studies Standard ▶ Identifies local officials

- ▶ Prepare a bulletin board with the desired color of craft paper, a border, and the title "Whooo Are the Leaders in This Town?"
- ▶ Enlarge the owl (p. 237) and trace it on white construction paper. Color and cut it out. Staple it on one side of the bulletin board.
- ▶ Duplicate an owl (p. 237) on white paper for each student.
- ▶ Challenge students to look through newspapers, magazines, and flyers to find pictures of local officials. Have them bring the pictures to school.
- ▶ Have students cut out an owl and color it. Have them write an official's name and job on their owl.
- ▶ Staple the owls and pictures to the bulletin board.

Content-Related Bulletin Board Ideas

194 Wise Owls Use Dictionaries

Language Arts Standard ▶ Uses resources to build word meanings

- Prepare a bulletin board with the desired color of craft paper, a border, and the title "Wise Owls Use Dictionaries."
- Enlarge the owl (p. 237) and trace it on white construction paper. Color and cut it out. Staple the owl to the center of the bulletin board.
- Duplicate the dictionary (p. 239) on white paper for each student. Have students cut out the dictionaries.
- Challenge students to listen at school and at home for unfamiliar words.
- Invite them to find the unfamiliar words in the dictionary and record the word and its meaning on a dictionary cut out.
- Allow each student to share the word before stapling it to the bulletin board.

195 A Wise Owl Feathers Its Nest

Math Standard ▶ Determines the value of a collection of coins

- Prepare a bulletin board with blue craft paper and the title "A Wise Owl Feathers Its Nest."
- Paint a large tree with a hole in it. Show part of an owl's nest in the hole.
- Duplicate an owl (p. 237), color it, and cut it out. Staple it on the tree.
- Paint six more nests in a pleasing arrangement around the tree. Number them from 1–6.
- Put different kinds of coins in several resealable bags. Staple the bags to the nests.
- Have students number a sheet of paper from 1–6.
- Have them count the coins and record the amount in each nest on their paper.
- Change the coins several times during the week.

196 Give a Hoot for the Environment!

Science Standard ▶ Describes strategies for protecting the environment

- Prepare a bulletin board with the desired color of craft paper, a border, and the title "Give a Hoot for the Environment."
- Enlarge the owl (p. 140) and trace it on white construction paper. Color and cut it out. Staple it to the center of the bulletin board.
- Discuss the ways that people can protect the environment.
- Then invite each student to make a poster showing one way he or she can help protect the environment.
- Staple the completed posters to the bulletin board.

Heroes

197 Puzzled by History Heroes

Social Studies Standard ▶ Identifies historical figures who have exemplified good citizenship

Materials

- craft paper
- border
- posters of famous, historic people
- sentence strips

- poster board
- straight blade knife
- stapler
- rubber cement
- markers

Teacher Preparation

- ▶ Prepare a bulletin board with the desired color of craft paper, a border, and the title "Puzzled by History Heroes."
- ▶ Use rubber cement to adhere each poster to a sheet of poster board.
- ▶ Cut each dried poster into six puzzle pieces.
- ▶ Write six clues about each person on separate sentence strips. Number the clues.
- ▶ Each day, staple a puzzle piece to the bulletin board, saving the largest portion of the face for the final piece.
- ▶ Read a clue each day and staple it to the bulletin board. Allow students to guess the mystery person's identity.

(page 31)

Additional Social Studies Bulletin Board Ideas

198 A "Heart-y" Hero Sandwich ✄

Social Studies Standard ▶ Identifies ordinary people who helped shape the community

- Prepare a bulletin board with the desired color of craft paper and the title "A 'Heart-y' Hero Sandwich."
- Enlarge the sandwich (p. 242) and trace the figure on white craft paper. Color and cut out the sandwich.
- Make templates of the heart (p. 243). Enlarge and cut out several hearts to use as backgrounds for magazine and newspaper articles.
- Invite students to trace hearts on red, pink, and white paper and cut them out.
- Then have students use the hearts to make a patterned border around the bulletin board.
- Cut out articles and pictures from magazines and newspapers that tell stories about people in the community who help others or who do heroic deeds.
- Gather students and staple the sandwich to the bulletin board.
- Explain that the sandwich is a hero sandwich and is also known as a submarine sandwich.
- Invite students to name characteristics of a hero, such as honest, hardworking, and brave. Write a characteristic on each layer of the sandwich.
- Share the magazine and newspaper articles and staple them to the bulletin board on a heart cutout.
- Challenge students to find other articles of other heroes to add to the bulletin board.
- Help students share their articles and staple them to the bulletin board on heart cutouts.

199 Heroic Headlines ✄✄✄

Social Studies Standard ▶ Identifies heroic deeds of state and national heroes and characters from folktales, legends, and myths

- Prepare a bulletin board with the desired color of craft paper and the title "Heroic Headlines." Unfold large sheets of newspaper and gather the ends. Staple the ends of the newspaper to the perimeter of the bulletin board to create a scalloped look.
- Enlarge the newspaper boy (p. 179) and trace the figure on white craft paper. Color and cut out the boy. Staple the figure on one side of the bulletin board.
- Duplicate a newspaper (p. 180) for each student.
- Invite students to choose a real or make-believe hero and imagine that they are writing a newspaper article about the person and the heroic deed.
- Discuss that the article should answer the questions *who, what, where, when, why,* and *how.*
- Challenge students to write a headline that will capture the readers' interest. Have them write the final draft on the newspaper and include a "photo" of the hero.
- Invite students to read their stories aloud before stapling the newspapers to the bulletin board in a pleasing arrangement.

Content-Related Bulletin Board Ideas

200 Sharing Sandwiches

Math Standard ▶ Names fractional parts of a whole object when given a concrete representation

- ▶ Prepare a bulletin board with the desired color of craft paper, a border, and the title "Sharing Sandwiches."
- ▶ Enlarge the newspaper boy (p. 179) and trace the figure, without the newspaper, on white craft paper. Color and cut out the boy. Staple the figure on one side of the bulletin board.
- ▶ Staple a file folder to one corner near the bottom of the bulletin board to make a pocket. Store the sandwich pieces in this pocket.
- ▶ Enlarge and duplicate seven sandwiches (p. 242). Color the sandwiches and cut them out.
- ▶ Glue one sandwich to the hand of the boy. Glue the remaining six sandwiches on poster board and cut them into halves, thirds, fourths, etc. to show different fractional patterns.
- ▶ Staple the sandwich parts together on the bulletin board at students' eye level, but leave off one part of each sandwich.
- ▶ Cut and fold six sentence strips to make pockets for each missing sandwich piece. Staple a pocket under each of the six sandwiches.
- ▶ Invite students to match the missing parts to the correct sandwiches and correctly name the fractional parts.

201 Serve Up a Sediment Sandwich

Science Standard ▶ Observes and describes differences in rocks

- ▶ Prepare a bulletin board with strips of fabrics and materials, including different colors of burlap, felt, and sandpaper, to resemble layers of sedimentary rock.
- ▶ Add a border and the title "Serve Up a Sediment Sandwich."
- ▶ Enlarge and duplicate a sandwich (p. 242) for each student.
- ▶ Lead students in a discussion about the characteristics of sedimentary rocks using the analogy of a sandwich with layers.
- ▶ Encourage students to make their own sediment sandwich using the same fabrics as the background on the bulletin board.
- ▶ Staple the completed sandwiches to the bulletin board.

Bulletin Boards, SV 1-4190-1884-1

Landforms and Water Bodies

202 One If by Land, and Two If by Sea ✂✂

Social Studies Standard ▶ Identifies major landforms and bodies of water, including continents and oceans

Materials

map pattern on page 244, blue craft paper, border, small paper plates, brown and white construction paper, straws, crayons or markers, scissors, glue, stapler, overhead projector

Teacher Preparation

▶ Prepare a bulletin board with blue craft paper, a border, and the title "One If by Land, and Two If by Sea."

▶ Enlarge the map (p. 244) and trace the continents on brown construction paper. Cut them out and staple them to the bulletin board.

▶ Cut straws in half. Provide two halves for each student.

▶ Cut white construction paper into 2" x 3" rectangles. Provide two rectangles for each student.

▶ Discuss the background of the famous Revolutionary War saying *One if by land and two if by sea* from Henry Wadsworth Longfellow's ballad "Paul Revere's Ride."

▶ Have students identify an ocean and staple their boat to that place. Have students identify a continent and staple their flag to that place.

Student Directions

Boat

▶ Color the back of a paper plate to look like a boat. Fold the plate in half with the white sides together. Cut a slit on the foldline in the very center of the boat.

▶ Slip a straw in the slit for the boat mast.

▶ Write *2* on a white rectangle. Glue the rectangle to the top of the straw to make a sail.

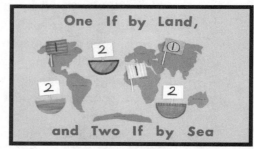

(page 31)

Flag

▶ Make a flag design on a white rectangle. Write *1* on the flag.

▶ Glue the flag to half of a straw.

Additional Social Studies Bulletin Board Ideas

203 Where Will You Live? ✂✂

Social Studies Standard ▶ **Identifies the physical characteristics of a place**

- ▶ Prepare a bulletin board with blue craft paper, a border, and the title "Where Will You Live?"
- ▶ Enlarge the United States map and key (p. 245) and trace them on white craft paper.
- ▶ Use a topography map as a guide to color the different features to match those on the map. For example, color the plains green and the rivers and lakes blue. Color the key accordingly.
- ▶ Duplicate a paper doll (p. 248) for each student. Invite students to color the figure to look like them and cut it out.
- ▶ Identify the different landforms and bodies of water for students. Point out the physical characteristics and environments of each.
- ▶ Invite students to choose one place they would like to live. Have them identify the feature and staple the paper doll to that area on the bulletin board.

204 Building Communities ✂✂✂

Social Studies Standard ▶ **Describes and explains variations in the physical environment**

- ▶ Prepare a bulletin board with white craft paper, a border, and the title "Building Communities."
- ▶ Make several templates of the folded house (p. 246). Have each student trace the house on a sheet of white paper
- ▶ Write the following words on chart paper: *mountain, plain, harbor, swamp, forest, river, lake, ocean.*
- ▶ Lead students in a discussion of the different landforms and bodies of water. Challenge students to name and identify other landforms and bodies of water. Write their responses on chart paper.
- ▶ Then have the students work cooperatively to plan a bulletin board showing a region that has all of the features listed on the chart paper.
- ▶ Have some students draw the entire area like a map and have others illustrate the individual features and paint the details. Encourage students to name the features creatively.
- ▶ Have students fold a house on the dotted line. Tell them to cut along the solid lines. Have students decorate and color the outside of the house by adding doors, windows, flowers, etc.
- ▶ Have students write a brief description on the inside of the house of where on the map they would build a house and why.
- ▶ Once students' houses are complete, lead students in a discussion of where people build communities and why.
- ▶ Invite students to tell where they would build a house. Then staple students' completed houses to the bulletin board in those areas.

Content-Related Bulletin Board Ideas

205 Capital Places We Know

Language Arts Standard ▶ **Uses basic capitalization correctly**

- ▶ Prepare a bulletin board with blue craft paper and a border.
- ▶ Enlarge the map and key (p. 245). Trace them on white craft paper.
- ▶ Use a topography map as a guide to color the different features on the map. Color the key accordingly.
- ▶ Add the title "Capital Places We Know" to the bulletin board.
- ▶ Number each area of the map. For example, write *1* on the Appalachian Mountains.
- ▶ Tell students to number a sheet of paper with as many numbers as there are features. Then have students use a topography map to find and write the names of the features. Remind them that the names are proper nouns and begin with a capital letter.
- ▶ Discuss students' answers. Then write the names of the features on sentence strips and attach them to the correct areas on the map.

206 High and Wide—Long and Far

Math Standard ▶ **Writes numbers to 999,999**

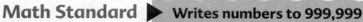

- ▶ Prepare a bulletin board with blue craft paper and a border.
- ▶ Enlarge the map (p. 244) and trace the continents on brown paper. Cut them out and staple them to the bulletin board.
- ▶ Add the title "High and Wide—Long and Far."
- ▶ Challenge students to research a fun number fact about a topographic feature in the world. For example, students can find the height of the highest mountain or the length of the longest river. Have them record the name and number on a card.
- ▶ Help students draw a representative symbol on the map and attach the card.

207 By the Clean Sea

Science Standard ▶ **Describes strategies for protecting the environment**

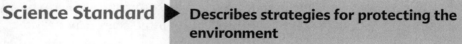

- ▶ Prepare a bulletin board with blue craft paper, a border, and the title "By the Clean Sea."
- ▶ Enlarge the map (p. 244) and trace the continents on brown paper. Cut them out and staple them to the bulletin board.
- ▶ Discuss environmental damages to the ocean and the different organisms that live in the ocean. Provide resources about endangered sea life, such as the sea turtles.
- ▶ Invite students to draw and color an organism that lives in the ocean. Then have students write a sentence that tells what people can do to keep the oceans clean.
- ▶ Staple students' completed work on the bulletin board.

Map Skills

208 "House" Your Town? ✂✂

Social Studies Standard ▶ **Creates and uses simple maps**

Materials

house pattern on page 246, town buildings patterns on page 247, paintbrush, pencils, green craft paper, black paint, border, transparency, overhead projector, white construction paper, sentence strips, scissors, stapler, crayons or markers, overhead projector

Teacher Preparation

- ▶ Prepare a bulletin board with the green craft paper.
- ▶ Use black paint to make roads that are perpendicular to each other.
- ▶ Add a border and the title "'House' Your Town?"
- ▶ Write familiar street names from your town or city on the roads.
- ▶ Duplicate a house (p. 246) on white construction paper for each student.
- ▶ Enlarge two copies of each of the town buildings (p. 247) on white paper. Color them and cut them out. Staple one set of buildings along the roads.
- ▶ Write *Key* on a sentence strip and staple it to the bulletin board. Staple the other set of buildings under the sentence strip to make a map key. Make a label for each building on a sentence strip.
- ▶ Draw a compass rose.
- ▶ Staple students' completed houses in the places they describe.
- ▶ Encourage pairs to give directions to each other so that a partner can trace the path with his or her finger.

Student Directions

- ▶ Fold a house on the dotted line. Cut along the solid lines. Color the outside of the house. Add details such as doors, windows, flowers, etc.
- ▶ Draw and color a special place inside your house. Draw a picture of yourself somewhere inside the house.
- ▶ Find a place on the map on the bulletin board to put your house. Describe the location using the words *north, south, east,* and *west.*

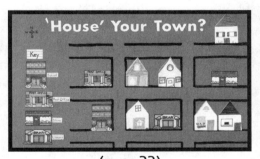

(page 32)

Additional Social Studies Bulletin Board Ideas

209 Me on the Map! ✀

Social Studies Standard ▶ **Uses terms to describe relative location**

- ▶ Prepare a bulletin board with green craft paper.
- ▶ Enlarge the road only (p. 198) without the house and paint the different parts of the scenery. Staple it to the bulletin board.
- ▶ Add a border and the title "Me on the Map!"
- ▶ Duplicate the town buildings (p. 247) on white paper. Color and cut them out. Staple the buildings along different roads.
- ▶ Duplicate a paper doll (p. 248) on white paper for each student. Cut out the dolls.
- ▶ Provide art supplies such as fabric, yarn, and markers and have students make a paper-doll image of themselves.
- ▶ Invite them to decide where they would like to place their doll on the map. Encourage them to use location words to describe the place.
- ▶ Staple the paper dolls to the places students describe.

210 A "Fair-ly" Fun Day ✀✀✀

Social Studies Standard ▶ **Identifies and uses the grid and symbols to locate places**

- ▶ Prepare a bulletin board with white craft paper and the title "A 'Fair-ly' Fun Day."
- ▶ Enlarge the fair grid map (p. 249) and trace everything in sections A2 and B2. Include the parking lot in B1 and the trees and benches in A1. Then paint the details.
- ▶ Duplicate the folded house (p. 246) and provide a small paper plate for each student.
- ▶ Invite students to choose to run a food booth or a game booth at the fair.
- ▶ Have students add details to the plate to make a food booth. Or have students fold the house on the dotted line and cut along the solid lines to make a game booth. Have them add details to the game booth.
- ▶ Help students staple their booths to the grid map.
- ▶ Invite students to plan a day at the fair. Have them make a list on a sheet of paper of the places they will visit and the grid they will be in at that time.
- ▶ Invite volunteers to share their list of places and explain how to use the grid map to locate the places.
- ▶ Staple students' completed papers on the bulletin board.

Content-Related Bulletin Board Ideas

211 At Home with the ABCs

Language Arts Standard ▶ Applies letter-sound correspondences

- ▶ Prepare a bulletin board with the desired color of craft paper, a border, and the title "At Home with the ABCs."
- ▶ Duplicate 26 houses (p. 246) on white paper. Distribute them to students.
- ▶ Make cards with the letters *a–z*. Put the cards in a bag.
- ▶ Have students fold a house on the dotted line and cut along the solid lines.
- ▶ Then ask them to select a letter card and write the partner letter on the front of their house.
- ▶ Challenge them to draw and color a picture on the inside of the house of something whose name begins with that letter sound.
- ▶ Have students line up in ABC order according to the letter on their house.
- ▶ Staple students' completed houses in ABC order on the bulletin board.

212 A Fair Way to Spend Money

Math Standard ▶ Uses a problem-solving model

- ▶ Prepare a bulletin board with the desired color of craft paper and the title "A Fair Way to Spend Money."
- ▶ Enlarge the fair grid map and the key (p. 249) on white craft paper. Color the map.
- ▶ Add the following information to the key: paddle boat—$3.00, drink—$1.00, hot dog—$2.00, game booth—$0.50, carnival ride—$1.00.
- ▶ Tell students to imagine they have $10.00 to spend at the fair. Have them make a list on a sheet of paper to tell how they will spend their money.
- ▶ Staple students' completed lists around the map.

Classroom Management

213 A Road Map for Good Behavior

- ▶ Prepare a bulletin board with green craft paper.
- ▶ Use black paint to make a road from the bottom left-hand corner to the top right-hand corner.
- ▶ Add a border and the title "A Road Map for Good Behavior."
- ▶ Duplicate the town buildings (p. 247) on white paper. Color them and cut them out. Staple the buildings along the road.
- ▶ Duplicate, color, and cut out a car (p. 202).
- ▶ Discuss with students a set of behavior goals and a small reward for achieving them.
- ▶ Write the goals on sentence strips and staple them to the road as a reminder.
- ▶ Move the car along the road as students meet the goals.

national Symbols

214 Be Proud of Your Flag ✂✂

Social Studies Standard ▶ **Identifies the flag as a national symbol**

Materials

- flag patterns on page 250
- map pattern on page 252
- craft paper
- sentence strips
- self-stick adhesive tape
- scissors
- stapler
- crayons or markers
- overhead projector

Teacher Preparation

▶ Prepare a bulletin board with the desired color of craft paper and the title "Be Proud of Your Flag."

▶ Duplicate the three flags (p. 250) for each student.

▶ Help them staple the flags in a pattern as a border.

▶ Enlarge the map of North America (p. 252) in the middle of the bulletin board. Color the map.

▶ Enlarge the three flags. Color and cut them out. Place self-stick adhesive tape on the back of each flag.

▶ Write a few phrases on sentence strips that describe the flags of Canada, the United States, and Mexico. Staple the phrases on the correct countries.

▶ Discuss with students how the colors and symbols on each country's flag are special.

Student Directions

▶ Color and cut out the Canadian, the United States, and the Mexican flags.

▶ Make a pattern border around the bulletin board with your flags.

▶ Read the phrases that describe each flag.

▶ Place each flag on the correct country.

(page 32)

Additional Social Studies Bulletin Board Ideas

215 We Love the Red, White, and Blue ✂

Social Studies Standard ▶ Identifies the United States flag

- ▶ Prepare a bulletin board with the desired color of craft paper, a border, and the title "We Love the Red, White, and Blue."
- ▶ Cut a large, rectangular piece of white craft paper that covers all of the bulletin board except for the border and the caption.
- ▶ Lay the paper on a table. Use a ruler to draw lines that designate the field of blue on the United States flag.
- ▶ Paint each student's hand blue. Have them press a handprint with fingers together on the designated area. Guide them to place handprints close together so that the area is mostly blue.
- ▶ Next paint the student's other hand red. Have students place their red handprints in rows to form the seven red stripes of the flag.
- ▶ Cut a sponge in a star shape. When the blue paint is dry, have students use a sponge to paint 50 stars on the field of blue.
- ▶ Staple the completed flag on the bulletin board below the title.

216 The Flip of a Coin ✂✂✂

Social Studies Standard ▶ Understands the origins of customs, including symbols

- ▶ Prepare a bulletin board with the desired color of craft paper, a border, and the title "The Flip of a Coin."
- ▶ Enlarge the Statue of Liberty, the bald eagle, the Liberty Bell, and Uncle Sam (p. 253). Color, cut them out, and staple them on the bulletin board.
- ▶ Lead a discussion with students about these American symbols and their importance.
- ▶ Explain to students that they have been selected to design a new coin. The coin must have an American symbol on it. Tell students that they may also use other symbols that are not on the bulletin board.
- ▶ Provide students with craft materials such as construction paper, paper plates, and markers or paints to use to design their coin.
- ▶ Challenge students to include a patriotic phrase on their coin and the year it was minted.
- ▶ Invite students to write a paragraph about the origins of each symbol they included.
- ▶ Staple students' coins and paragraphs on the bulletin board in a pleasing arrangement.

Content-Related Bulletin Board Ideas

217 Symbolic Sentences

Language Arts Standard ▶ **Uses nouns and verbs in sentences**

- Prepare a bulletin board with the desired color of craft paper, a border, and the title "Symbolic Sentences."
- Enlarge the American flag (p. 250), the White House (p. 251), and the American symbols (p. 253). Color and cut them out. Then staple them on the bulletin board in a pleasing arrangement. Label each of the symbols.
- Invite students to use each symbol in a sentence. Have them write their sentence on a sentence strip.
- Staple students' sentences on the bulletin board.

218 Measure the White House

Math Standard ▶ **Estimates and measures length using nonstandard units**

- Prepare a bulletin board with the desired color of craft paper, a border, and the title "Measure the White House."
- Enlarge the White House (p. 251) to a width of three or four feet. Cut it out and staple it in the middle of the bulletin board.
- Have students estimate how many interlocking cubes wide the White House is. Then have them write their name and their guess on an index card.
- Staple the cards on the bulletin board next to the White House.
- When all students have made their guess, invite them to measure the White House with interlocking cubes to find the width.
- Write the width on the White House.
- Encourage students to determine whose guess was the closest to the correct width.

Classroom Management

219 Uncle Sam Wants You to Be a Good Worker

- Prepare a bulletin board with the desired color of craft paper, a border, and the title "Uncle Sam Wants You to be a Good Worker."
- Enlarge the Uncle Sam (p. 253). Color, cut it out, and staple it in the middle of the bulletin board.
- Duplicate a United States flag (p. 250) for each student. Have students color and cut out their flag. Then have them write their name on it.
- Staple a student's flag on the bulletin board in a pleasing arrangement when he or she exhibits a designated work skill.

Fish Patterns

Use with "Fishin' for Definitions" on page 33, "Get Hooked on the ABCs" on page 34, "Putting Words in 'Alpha-bait-ical' Order" on page 34, "The One That Got Away" on page 35, "Let's Make It 'Of-fish-al'!" on page 35, "We're Catching On to Good Behavior" on page 35, "Fishing for Numbers" on page 94, and "Feathers, Fur, or Scales" on page 106.

Worm Pattern

Use with "Fishin' for Definitions" on page 33.

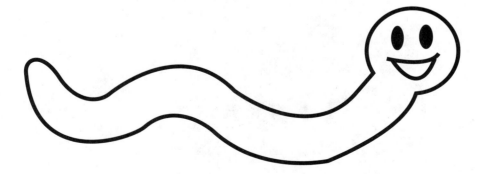

Bulletin Boards, SV 1-4190-1884-1

Girl Fishing Pattern

Use with "Putting Words in 'Alpha-bait-ical' Order" on page 34 and "We're Catching On to Good Behavior" on page 35.

Ice-Cream Label Patterns

Use with "Cool Flavors of Books" on page 36.

Pepper-myth

Cookies and Poems

Rocky Road
Biography

Neapolitan Nonfiction

Story-berry

Tall Tale Toffee

Cone and Scoop of Ice Cream Patterns

Use with "Cool Flavors of Books" on page 36, "Sweet Treat Books" on page 37, "Cooling Off on a Hot Day!" on page 38, and "We All Scream for Ice Cream!" on page 38.

Bulletin Boards, SV 1-4190-1884-1

Girl with Ice Cream Pattern

Use with "Cooling Off on a Hot Day!" on page 38.

Circus Animals Patterns

Use with "The Circus Is in Town" on page 39, "Big Sentences Under the Big Top" on page 40, "'An-noun-cing' the Circus Fun" on page 40, "Balls of Fun" on page 41, and "Horsing Around with Number Sentences" on page 69.

Announcer Pattern

Use with "'An-noun-cing' the Circus Fun" on page 40 and "Ticket Time" on page 41.

Engine Pattern

Use with "The Circus Is in Town" on page 39 and "Stay on Track with Contractions" on page 98.

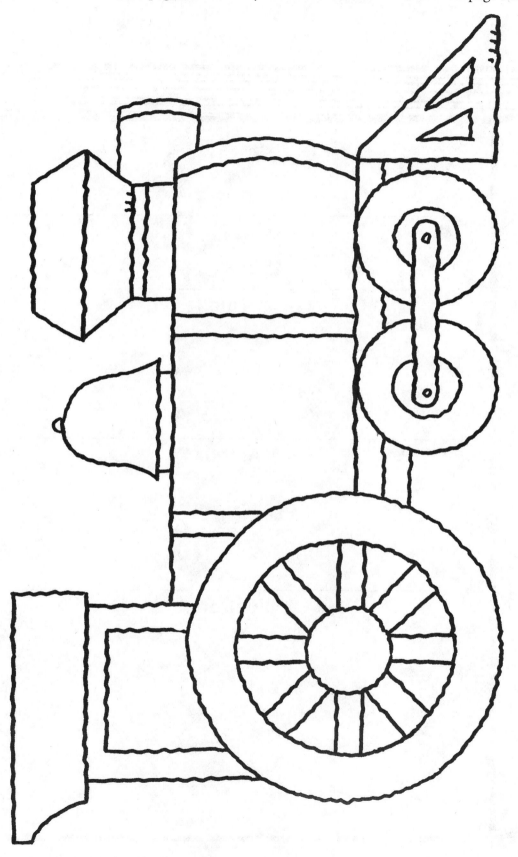

Book Cover Pattern

Use with "Terrific Titles, Awesome Authors, and Illustrious Illustrators" on page 42 and "The Total Points of the Title" on page 44.

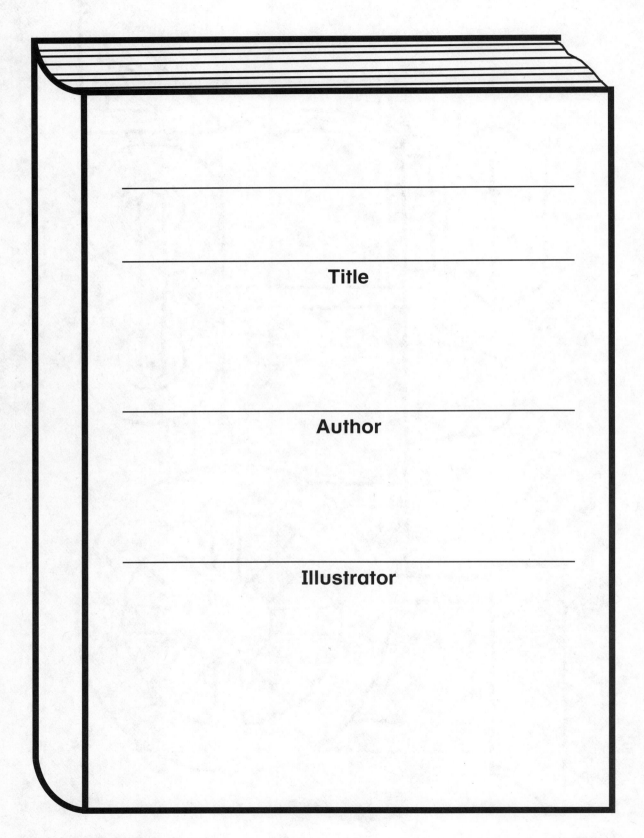

Title

Author

Illustrator

Bulletin Boards, SV 1-4190-1884-1

Open Book Pattern

Use with "Know Where to Look in a Book" on page 43 and "Reading Up on Skeletons" on page 44.

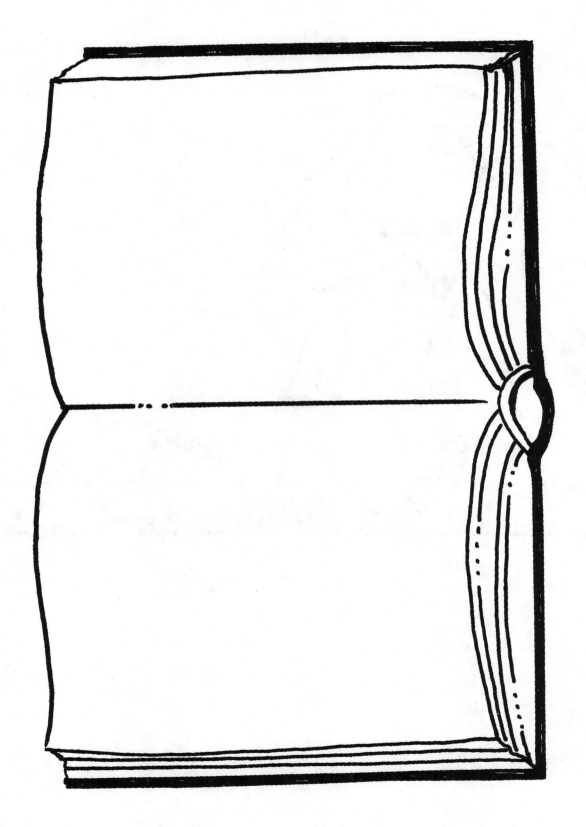

Girl Talking on the Phone Pattern

Use with "On the Phone with Phonics" on page 45 and "Let's Talk About Plants" on page 47.

Bulletin Boards, SV 1-4190-1884-1

Cell Phone Pattern

Use with "Text Message a Digraph Clue" on page 46.

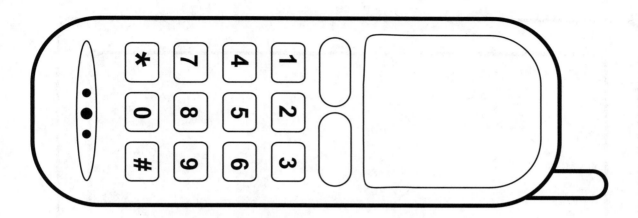

Telephone Patterns

Use with "The Phone 'Consonant-ly' Rings" on page 46, "Dialing for Dollars" on page 47, and "Telephone or Computer" on page 47.

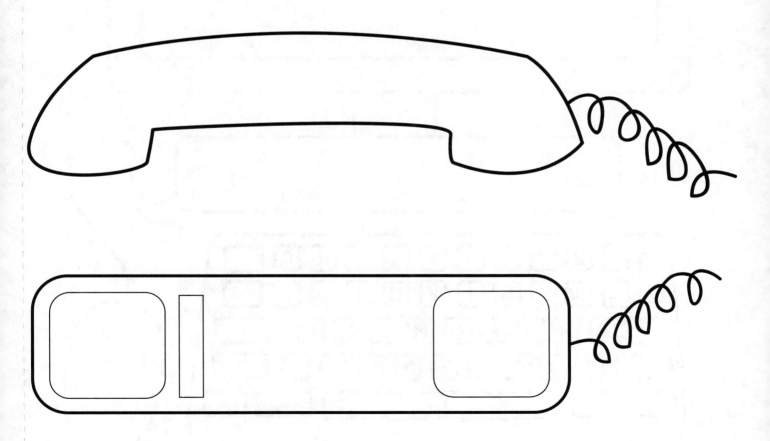

Computer Pattern

Use with "Telephone or Computer" on page 47.

Animal Face Patterns

Use with "Doggone Good Sentences" on page 48 and "Baa, Baa, Woolly Sheep" on page 71.

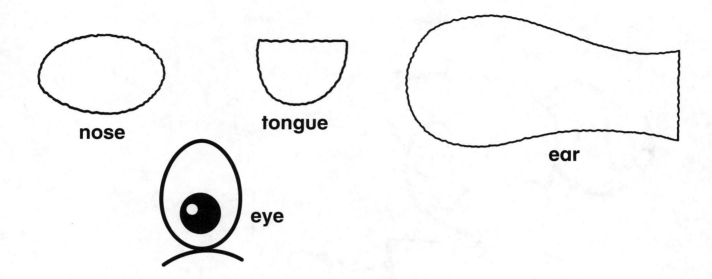

nose

tongue

ear

eye

Dog Pattern

Use with "Big Sentences Under the Big Top" on page 40, "'An-noun-cing' the Circus Fun" on page 40, "I 'Spot' a Sentence!" on page 49, "Home, Sweet Home" on page 50, and "'Spotting' Fractions" on page 50.

Girl and Dog Pattern

Use with "I 'Spot' a Sentence!" on page 49 and "'Paws' for Commas" on page 49.

Bulletin Boards, SV 1-4190-1884-1

Doghouse Pattern

Use with "Home, Sweet Home" on page 50.

Paw Print Pattern

Use with "'Paws' for Commas" on page 49.

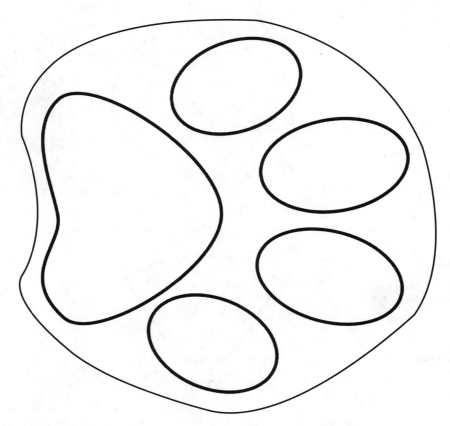

Lion Pattern

Use with "The Circus Is in Town" on page 39, "Big Sentences Under the Big Top" on page 40, "'An-noun-cing' the Circus Fun" on page 40, "Hunting for the Facts" on page 52, "Asking the King of the Jungle" on page 53, "Family Pride" on page 53, and "Feathers, Fur, or Scales" on page 106.

Lion Face Patterns

Use with "Here's the 'Mane' Idea" on page 51 and "Tell a Tale" on page 52.

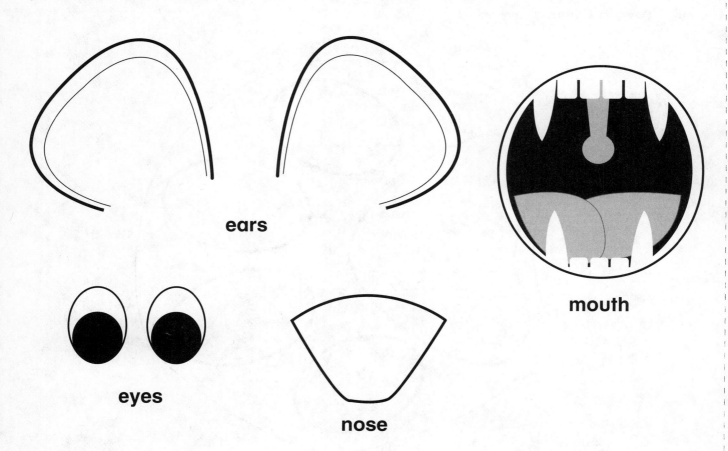

ears

eyes

nose

mouth

Bulletin Boards, SV 1-4190-1884-1

The Lion and Mouse Picture Cards

Use with "Tell a Tale" on page 52.

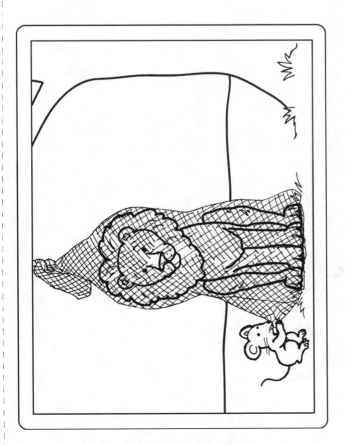

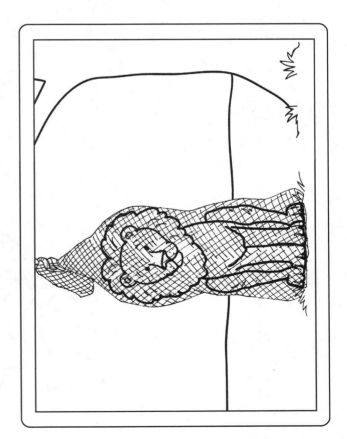

Spider Pattern

Use with "Spiders Are Good Researchers . . . They Make Webs!" on page 54 and "We Spin Good Questions" on page 55.

Fly Pattern

Use with "We Spin Good Questions" on page 55 and "Going to Great Lengths to Catch Flies" on page 81.

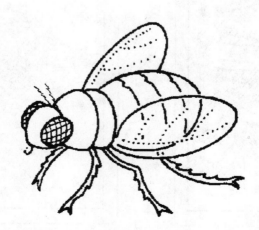

Spider Body Pattern

Use with "'Spider-ific' Facts" on page 55, "Spiders Are Everywhere!" on page 56, and "We 'Spy-der' Legs!" on page 56.

Pattern
Bulletin Boards, SV 1-4190-1884-1

Hat Pattern

Use with "The Cat's Hat Is Full of Rhymes" on page 57, "Dr. Seuss Is on the Loose" on page 58, and "Hats Off to Good Citizens" on page 59.

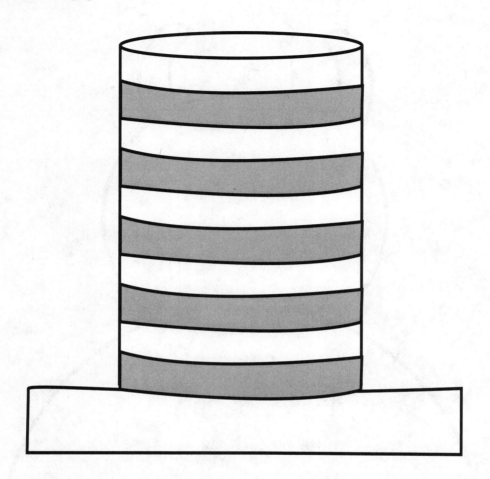

Egg with Yolk Pattern

Use with "Serving Up Rhyming Words" on page 58 and "Our Writing Is 'Egg-ceptional'" on page 59.

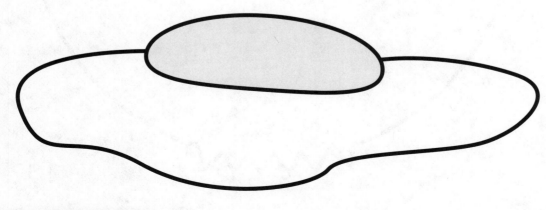

Cat Pattern

Use with "The Cat's Hat Is Full of Rhymes" on page 57 and "Numbers Are More or Less 'Purr-fect'" on page 59.

Ham Pattern

Use with "Serving Up Rhyming Words" on page 58.

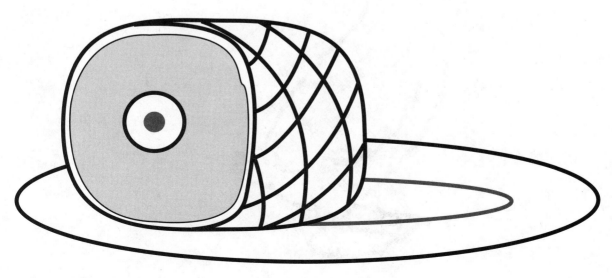

Cracked Egg and Eggshell Patterns

Use with "Take a Crack at Plurals" on page 60, "Building Our Families" on page 61, "What an Odd Duck!" on page 62, and "Be 'Eggs-tra' Sure About Your Measurements" on page 62.

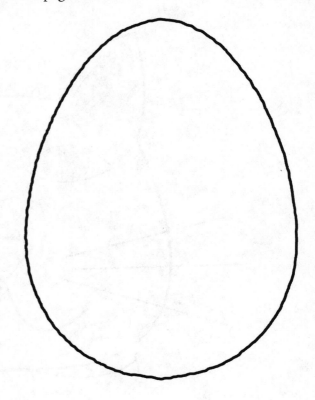

Walking Duck Pattern

Use with "'Waddle' We Do with Homonyms?" on page 61.

Duck Body and Wing Patterns

Use with "Building Our Families" on page 61, "What an Odd Duck!" on page 62, and "We're Not Ducking Our Responsibility" on page 62.

Carpenter Pattern

Use with "Look How We 'Fix' Words" on page 63, "Building Word Power" on page 64, "How 'Wood' You Order?" on page 65, and "Go to Great Lengths" on page 137.

Board and Nail Patterns

Use with "Look How We 'Fix' Words" on page 63, "How 'Wood' You Order?" on page 65, and "Go to Great Lengths" on page 137.

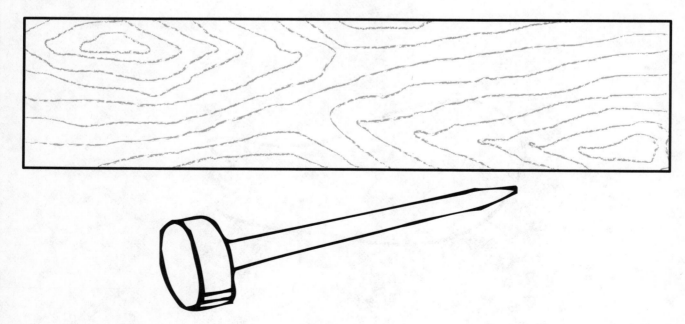

Bricklayer

Use with "Words to Build On" on page 64 and "Handy Helpers" on page 65.

Handprint Pattern

Use with "Handy Helpers" on page 65.

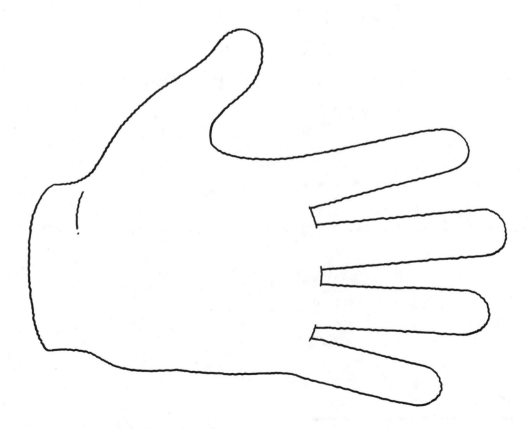

Word Page Pattern

Use with "Building Word Power" on page 64.

Word _____

Meaning A

fold _

Meaning B

Answer _____

Newspaper Boy Pattern

Use with "Read All About It" on page 66, "Steps to Good Citizenship" on page 95, "Heroic Headlines" on page 142, and "Sharing Sandwiches" on page 143.

Newspaper Pattern

Use with "Delivering the News" on page 68 and "Heroic Headlines" on page 142.

Barn Pattern

Use with "Horsing Around with Number Sentences" on page 69 and "Look for 'Sum' 'Differences' in This Herd" on page 70.

Farmer Pattern

Use with "It's Time to Plant!" on page 70, "Old MacDonald Goes to Work" on page 71, and "Making a Cake Is a Farm 'Product-ion'" on page 77.

Cow Pattern

Use with "Look for 'Sum' 'Differences' in This Herd" on page 70, "Look at This 'Moo-velous' Work!" on page 71, and "Making a Cake Is a Farm 'Product-ion'" on page 77.

Pattern
Bulletin Boards, SV 1-4190-1884-1

Monkey and Banana Patterns

Use with "Numbers by the Bunch" on page 72, "Swinging in Order" on page 73, "Monkeying Around with Numbers" on page 73, "We Are Curious About Seeds" on page 74, "Here's the Scoop on the Troop" on page 74, "Going Bananas over Good Behavior" on page 74, and "Feathers, Fur, or Scales" on page 106.

Tree Pattern

Use with "Monkeying Around with Numbers" on page 73, "We Are Curious About Seeds" on page 74, "Here's the Scoop on the Troop" on page 74, and "Going Bananas over Good Behavior" on page 74.

Joined Squares Pattern

Use with "We're 'Halving' a Colorful Cake!" on page 75.

Pattern
Bulletin Boards, SV 1-4190-1884-1

Pizza Pattern

Use with "It's a Pizza 'Part-y'!" on page 76.

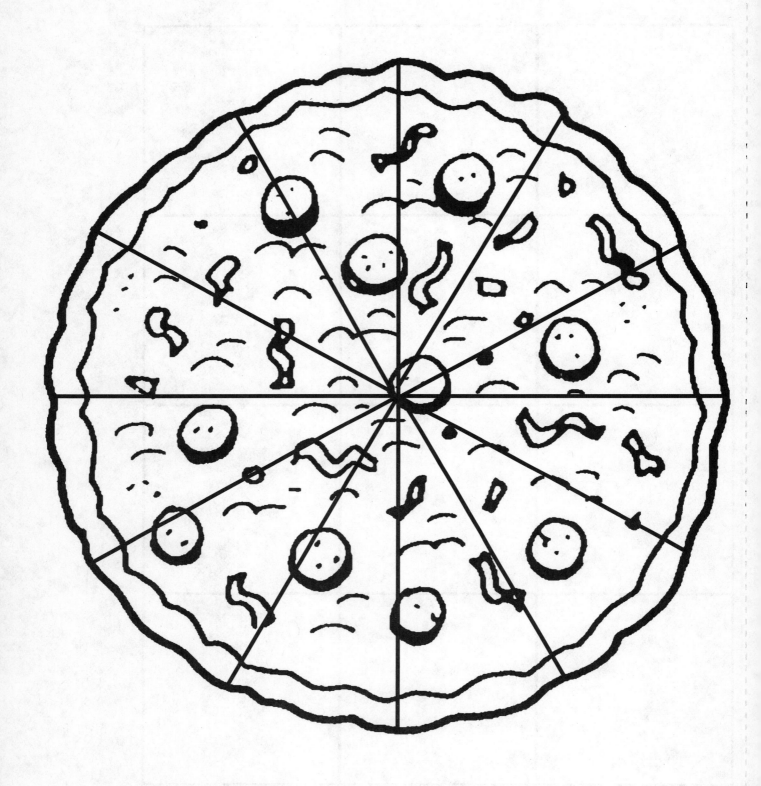

Pattern
Bulletin Boards, SV 1-4190-1884-1

Cake Pattern

Use with "We're 'Halving' a Colorful Cake!" on page 75 and "Making a Cake Is a Farm 'Product-ion'" on page 77.

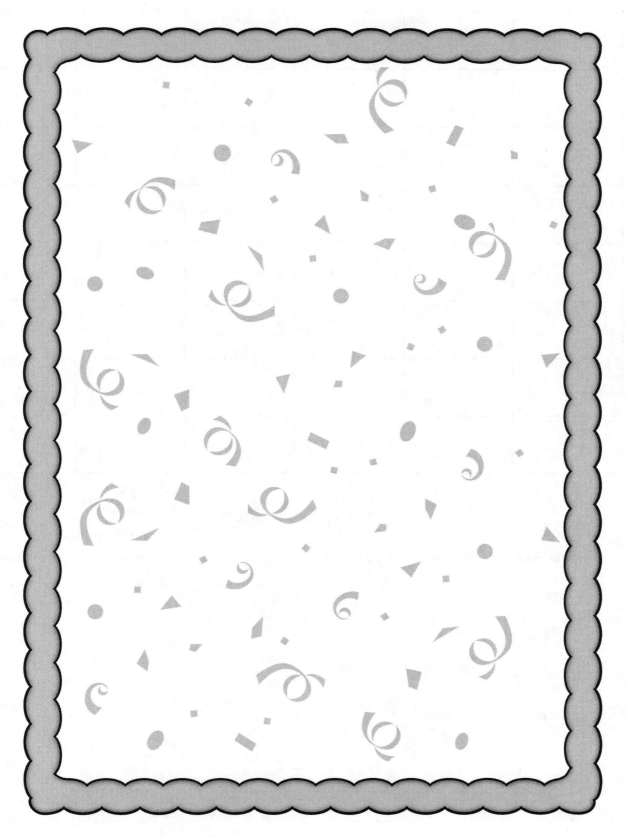

Bulletin Boards, SV 1-4190-1884-1

Bird Grid Pattern

Use with "Birds Are New at the Zoo" on page 79.

8						
7						
6						
5						
4						
3						
2						
1						
	owls	eagles	parrots	swans	penguins	flamingos

Bird Patterns

Use with "Our Favorite Feathered Friends" on page 78, "Birds Are New at the Zoo" on page 79, and "Feathers, Fur, or Scales" on page 106.

Frog Pattern

Use with "Going to Great Lengths to Catch Flies!" on page 81, "Frog on a Log" on page 82, "Lily Pad Leap" on page 82, "Grow, Frog, Grow!" on page 83, and "Hop to It, Frog!" on page 83.

Lily Pad Pattern

Use with "Lily Pad Leap" on page 82 and "Hop to It, Frog!" on page 83.

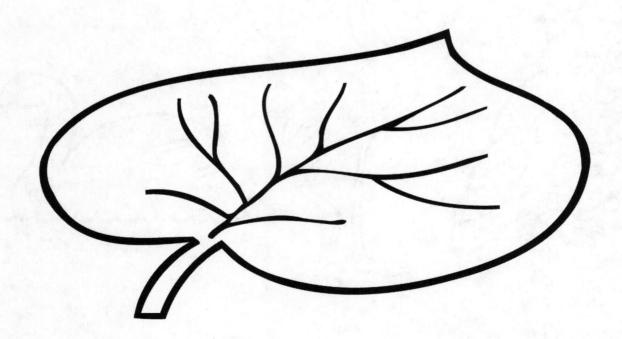

Tadpole Patterns

Use with "Grow, Frog, Grow!" on page 83.

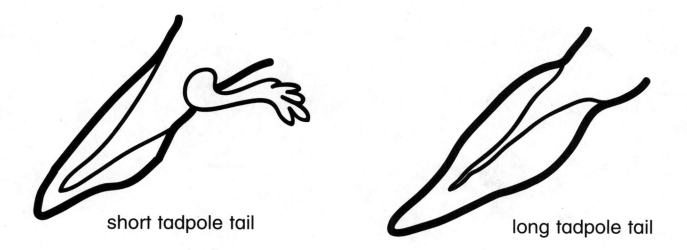

short tadpole tail

long tadpole tail

Bone Pattern

Use with "Doggone Good Sentences" on page 48.

Money Patterns

Use with "Dialing for Dollars" on page 47, "How Much Is That Toy in the Window?" on page 84, "A Penny Is Just a Penny" on page 85, "A 'Cents-able' Budget" on page 86, and "To the Market We Go" on page 113.

Coin Purse Pattern

Use with "Making 'Cents' of It All" on page 85.

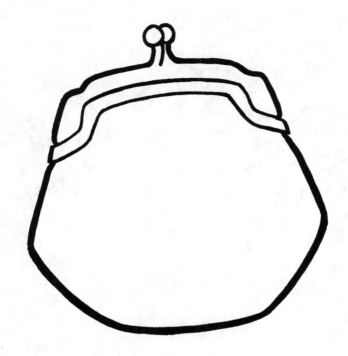

Piggy Bank Pattern

Use with "A Penny Is Just a Penny" on page 85 and "Bank on These Words" on page 86.

Ant Patterns

Use with "Pesky Picnic Ants" on page 87.

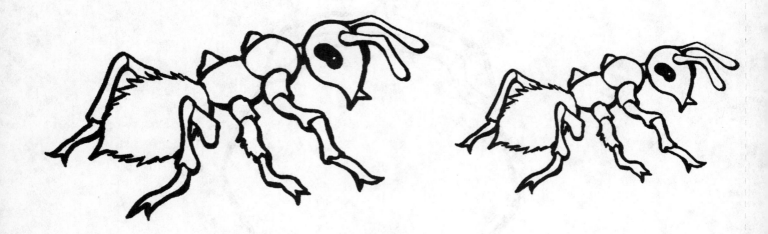

Butterfly Pattern

Use with "Flying Through Number Patterns" on page 88, "Bugs Can Be a Problem" on page 88, and "From Egg to Butterfly Growth Patterns" on page 89.

100s Number Chart

Use with "Flying Through Number Patterns" on page 88.

1	2	3	4	5	6	7	8	9	10
11	12	13	14	15	16	17	18	19	20
21	22	23	24	25	26	27	28	29	30
31	32	33	34	35	36	37	38	39	40
41	42	43	44	45	46	47	48	49	50
51	52	53	54	55	56	57	58	59	60
61	62	63	64	65	66	67	68	69	70
71	72	73	74	75	76	77	78	79	80
81	82	83	84	85	86	87	88	89	90
91	92	93	94	95	96	97	98	99	100

Pattern

Bulletin Boards, SV 1-4190-1884-1

Large Ladybug Pattern

Use with "Going Buggy over VCE Words" on page 89.

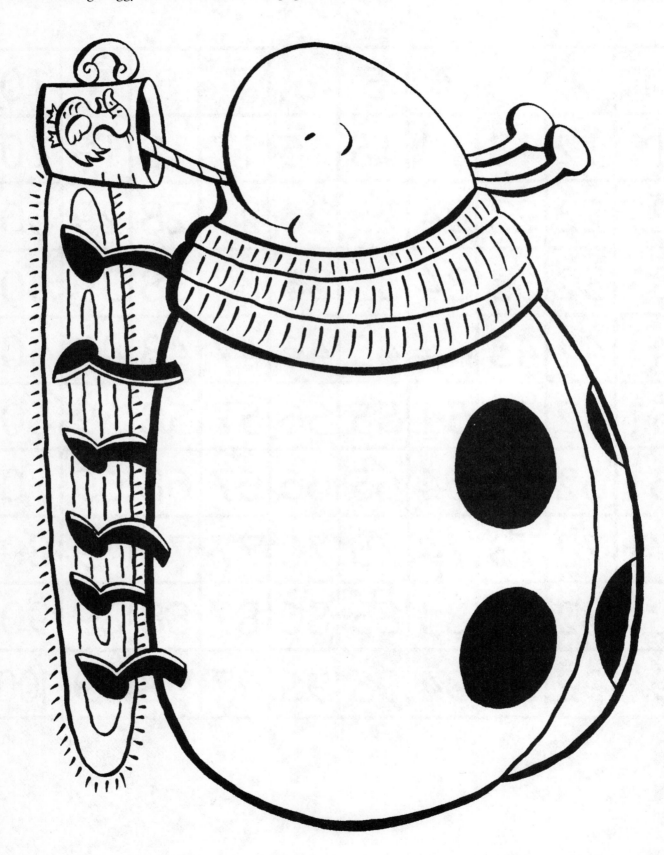

Pattern
Bulletin Boards, SV 1-4190-1884-1

Gum Ball Dispenser Pattern

Use with "Gum Ball Guessing" on page 91, "'Bubble-icious' Blends" on page 92, and "Sticking to Good Behavior" on page 92.

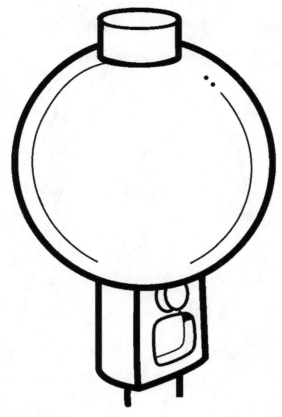

Small Ladybug Pattern

Use with "Flying Through Number Patterns" on page 88 and "Bugs Can Be a Problem" on page 88.

Road Pattern

Use with "Ready! Set! Roll!" on page 91, "'Wheel-y' Fun Facts" on page 92, and "Me on the Map!" on page 148.

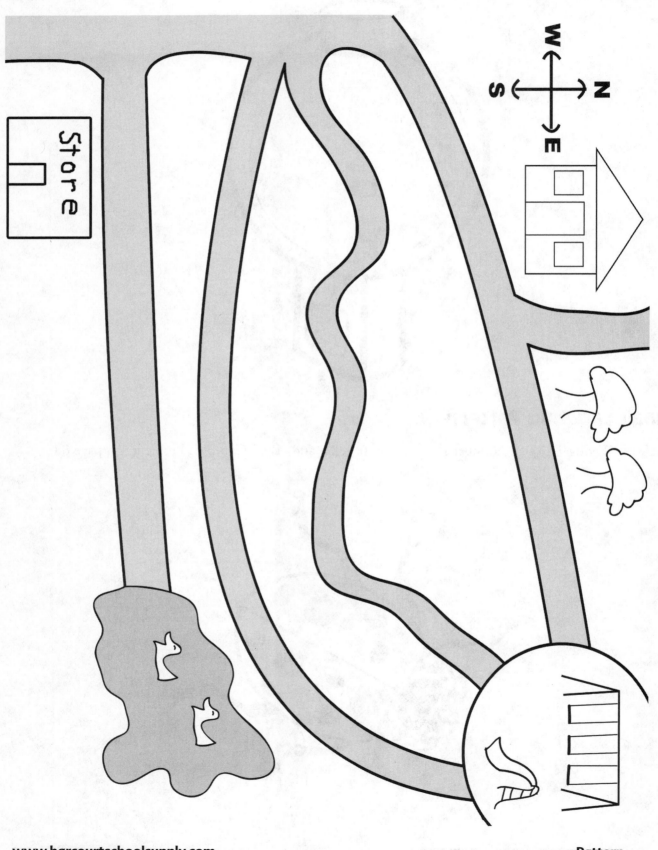

Detective Pattern

Use with "Clue Us In!" on page 93, "Toying Around with Problems" on page 94, "Fishing for Numbers" on page 94, and "The Case of the Missing Letters" on page 95.

Magnifying Glass Pattern

Use with "We Are Curious About Seeds" on page 74, "Clue Us In!" on page 93, "The Case of the Missing Letters" on page 95, and "Take a Closer Look at Your World" on page 95.

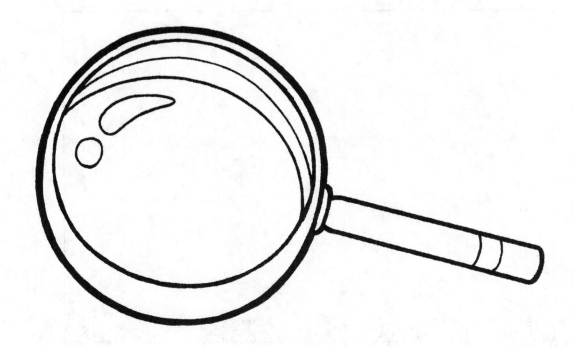

Footstep Pattern

Use with "Clue Us In!" on page 93 and "Steps to Good Citizenship" on page 95.

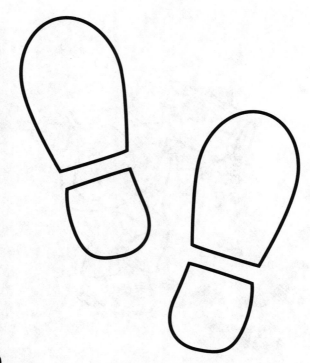

Aquarium Pattern

Use with "Fishing for Numbers" on page 94.

Toy Patterns

Use with "How Much Is That Toy in the Window?" on page 84 and "Toying Around with Problems" on page 94.

Car Pattern

Use with "Open the Door for Shapes" on page 96 and "A Road Map for Good Behavior" on page 149.

Shape Patterns

Use with "The Circus Is in Town" on page 39, "Balls of Fun" on page 41, "Spiders Are Good Researchers . . . They Make Webs!" on page 54, "Gum Ball Guessing" on page 91, "'Bubble-icious' Blends" on page 92, "Open the Door for Shapes" on page 96, "Sailing Along with Shapes" on page 97, and "Shape Up!" on page 98.

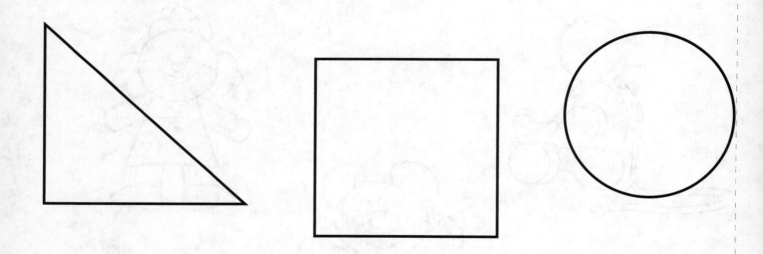

Truck Pattern

Use with "Trucks Only in This Area" on page 97.

Caboose and Boxcar Patterns

Use with "Stay on Track with Contractions" on page 98.

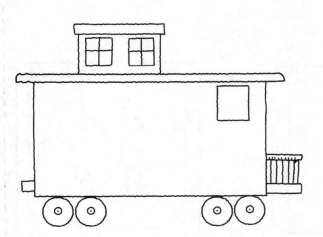

Gingerbread Man Pattern

Use with "I Can Sort, Too. I Can. I Can." on page 99, "Baking with Color" on page 100, "Sort, Sort, As Fast as You Can" on page 100, "Catch Me If You Can" on page 101, and "Running North, South, East, or West" on page 101.

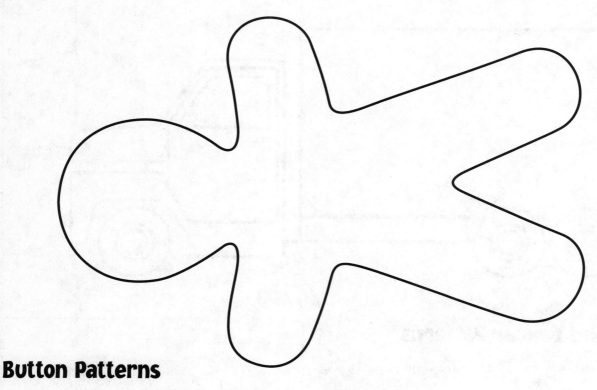

Button Patterns

Use with "Sort, Sort, As Fast as You Can" on page 100.

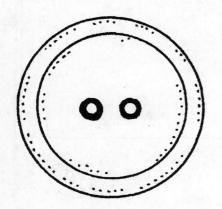
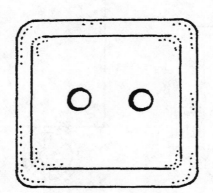
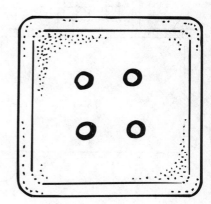

Geometric Solids Picture Cards

Use with "I Can Sort, Too. I Can. I Can." on page 99.

Hive Cell Pattern

Use with "It's Time to Get 'Buzzy'!" on page 102, "A Busy Word Hive" on page 104, and "Get the Facts on Bees" on page 104.

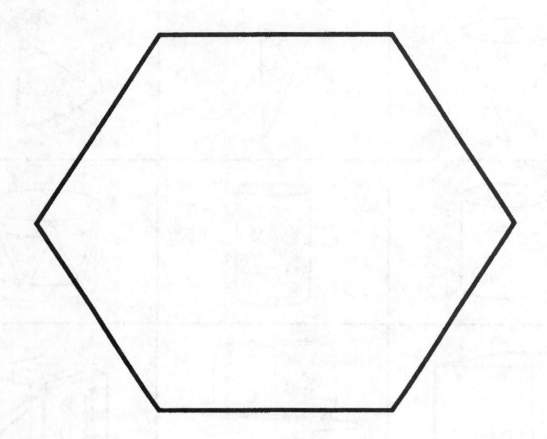

Bee Pattern

Use with "Bugs Can Be a Problem" on page 88, "It's Time to Get 'Buzzy'!" on page 102, "We Are Busy Bees!" on page 103, "Handy Clock Advice for Bees" on page 103, "A Busy Word Hive" on page 104, "Get the Facts on Bees" on page 104, and "'Bee' Safe—Use the Right Equipment" on page 121.

Clock Face Pattern

Use with "It's Time to Get 'Buzzy'!" on page 102, "Handy Clock Advice for Busy Bees" on page 103, and "Let's Rock Around the Clock" on page 119.

Digital Clock Pattern

Use with "Handy Clock Advice for Busy Bees" on page 103.

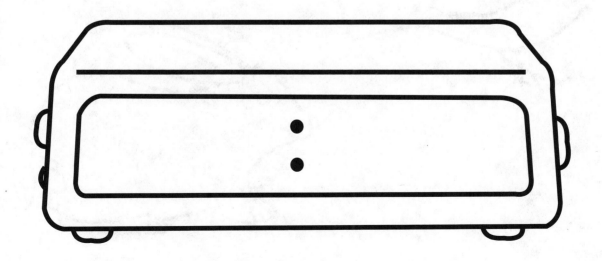

Animal Patterns

Use with "Feathers, Fur, or Scales" on page 106 and "Some 'Bunny' Is Hiding!" on page 107.

Animal Collage Pattern

Use with "Amazing Animal Riddles" on page 107.

Lunch Box Pattern

Use with "Lunch with the 'Three Rs'" on page 108 and "Mission Nutrition" on page 112.

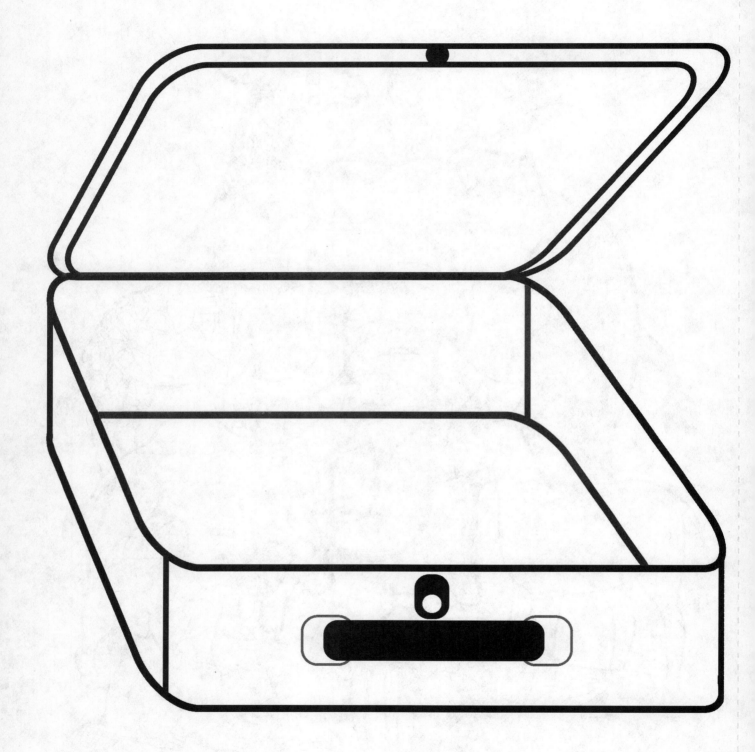

Earth Pattern

Use with "Wanted: A Clean, Healthy Planet" on page 109 and "Recycle These Letters into Words" on page 110.

Smog Scene Pattern

Use with "Past, Present, Future" on page 110.

Trash Pictures

Use with "Reuse the Refuse" on page 110.

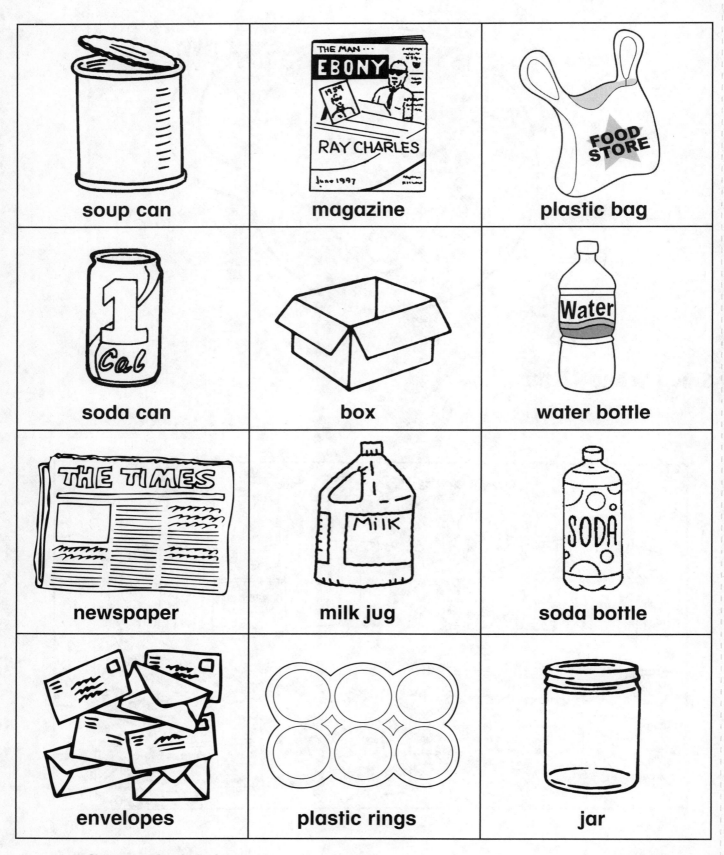

soup can	magazine	plastic bag
soda can	box	water bottle
newspaper	milk jug	soda bottle
envelopes	plastic rings	jar

Patterns
Bulletin Boards, SV 1-4190-1884-1

Food Pictures

Use with "A Nutritious Meal" on page 111, "Mission Nutrition" on page 112, "Grouping the Foods on the Pyramid" on page 112, and "To the Market We Go" on page 113.

bread	**carrot**	**yogurt**
cereal	**cheese**	**chicken**
noodles	**broccoli**	**egg**
fish	**ham**	**milk**

   Bulletin Boards, SV 1-4190-1884-1

Food Pictures (continued)

Use with "Mission Nutrition" on page 112, "Grouping the Foods on the Pyramid" on page 112, "Going Graphic over Food" on page 113, and "To the Market We Go" on page 113.

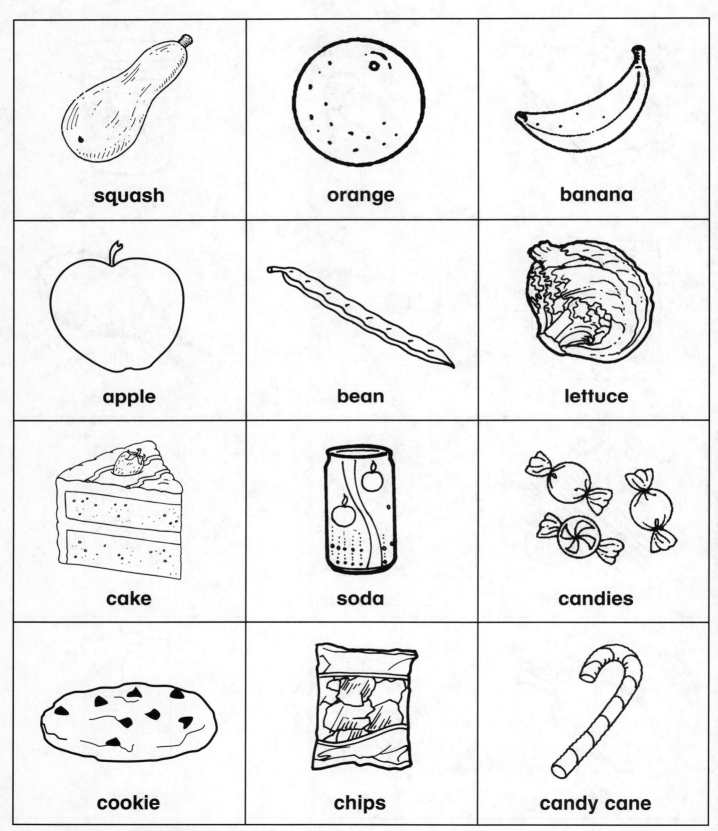

squash	**orange**	**banana**
apple	**bean**	**lettuce**
cake	**soda**	**candies**
cookie	**chips**	**candy cane**

www.harcourtschoolsupply.com
© Harcourt Achieve Inc. All rights reserved.

214

Patterns
Bulletin Boards, SV 1-4190-1884-1

Food Pyramid

Use with "Grouping the Foods on the Pyramid" on page 112.

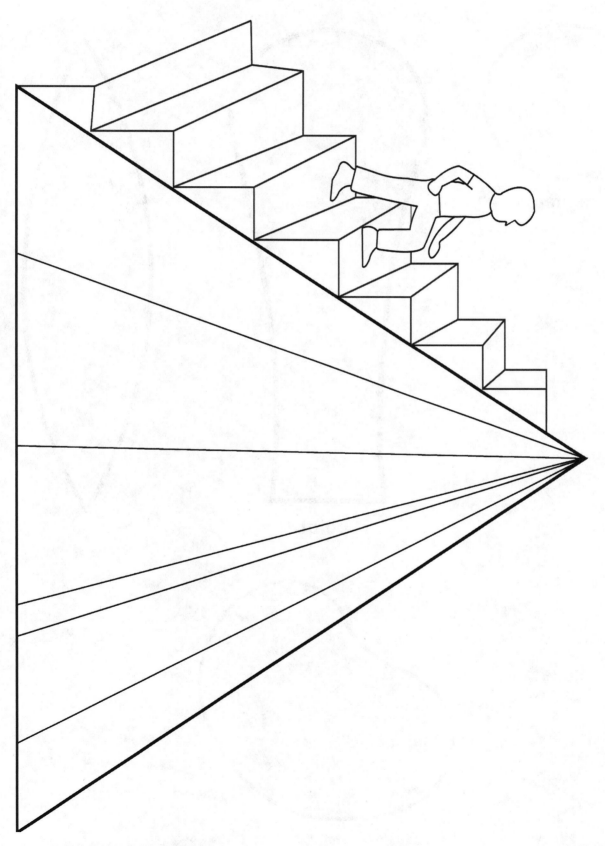

Flower Patterns

Use with "'Seed' Us Grow!" on page 114 and "Branching Out with Words" on page 116.

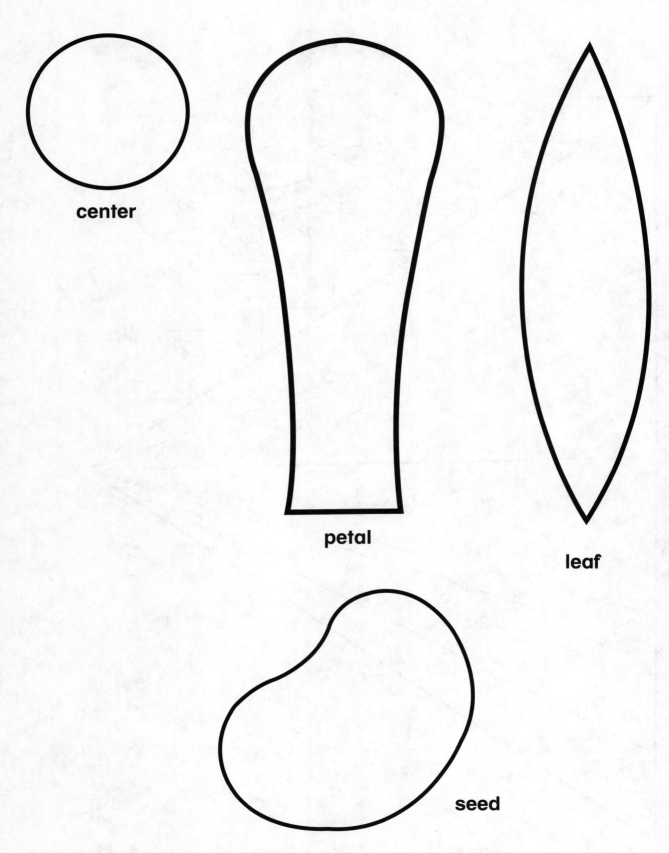

center

petal

leaf

seed

Bulletin Boards, SV 1-4190-1884-1

Girl Watering Pattern

Use with "A Handy Flower Garden" on page 116.

Rock Pattern

Use with "Rocks Have Minerals" on page 117, "As Hard as a Rock" on page 118, "Our Word Wall Rocks" on page 119, "Let's Rock Around the Clock" on page 119, and "We 'Lava' Good Listeners" on page 119.

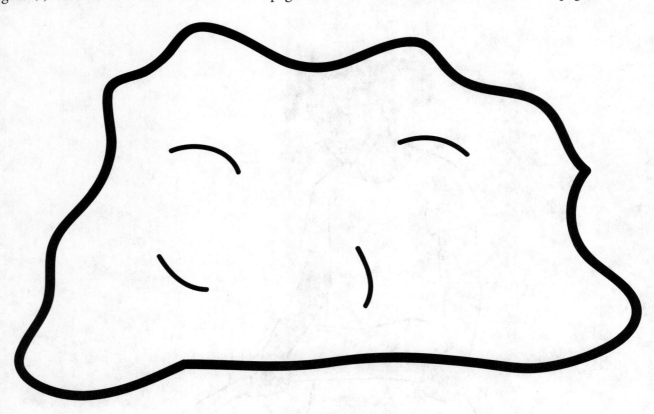

Scoop Pattern

Use with "Scoop Up a Good Book" on page 37.

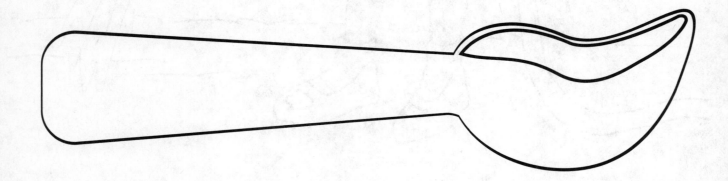

Volcano Pattern

Use with "We 'Lava' Good Listeners" on page 119.

Telephone Pattern

Use with "HELP! Call 911!" on page 122.

Telephone Information Pattern

Use with "HELP! Call 911!" on page 122.

Name

Address

Phone Number

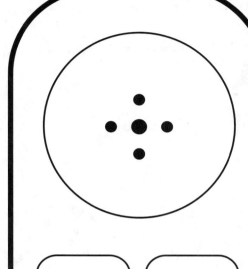

Safe Pattern

Use with "Safe in the Community" on page 122.

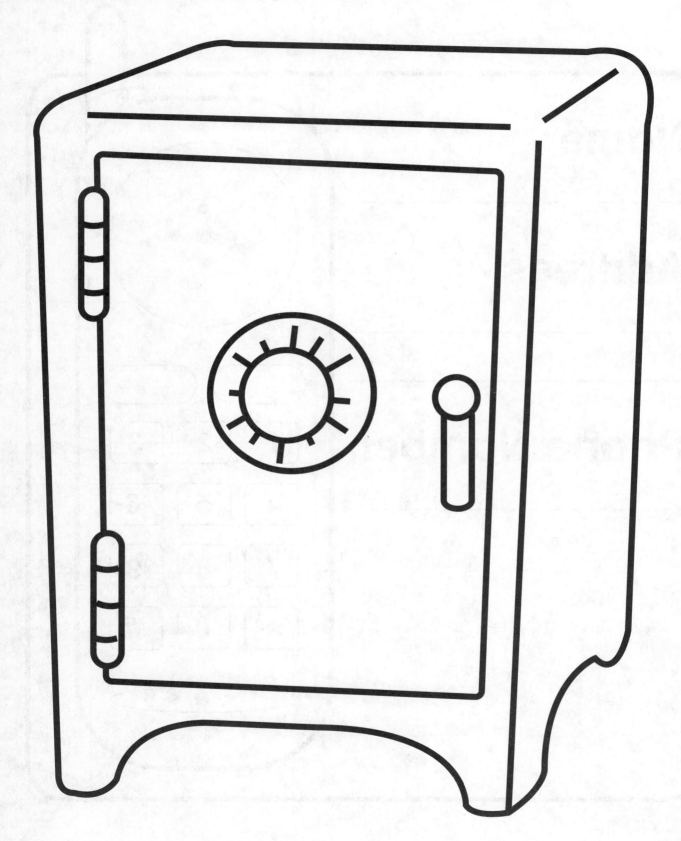

Planet Cards

Use with "A Group 'Plan-et' Project" on page 124.

Mercury

Venus

Earth

Mars

Uranus

Jupiter

Saturn

Neptune

Pluto

Star Pattern

Use with "Blasting Off to the Stars" on page 125 and "We're Patrolling for Good Workers" on page 137.

Fin Pattern

Use with "Blasting Off to the Stars" on page 125.

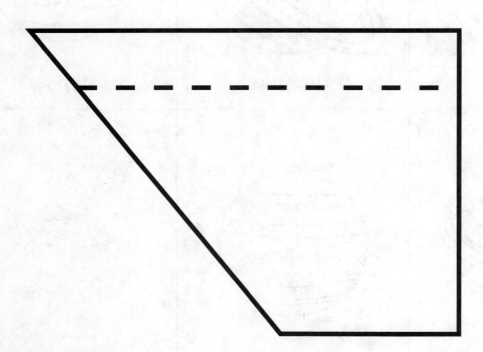

Nose Cone Pattern

Use with "Blasting Off to the Stars" on page 125.

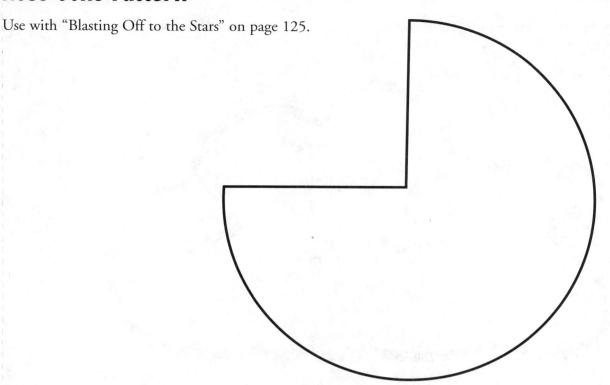

Sun Pattern

Use with "A Group 'Plan-et' Project" on page 124.

Cloud Pattern

Use with "Recycle These Letters into Words" on page 110, "Name That Cloud" on page 126, "Dropping In on Blends" on page 128, and "The Sky's the Limit" on page 128.

Raindrop Pattern

Use with "The Ups and Downs of the Water Cycle" on page 127, "Dropping in on Blends" on page 128, and "A Shower of Shapes" on page 128.

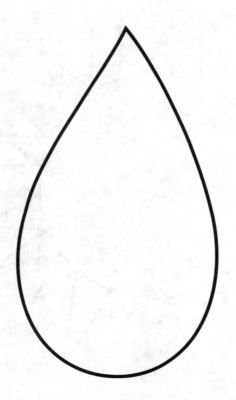

Umbrella Pattern

Use with "A Shower of Shapes" on page 128.

Water Cycle Pattern

Use with "The Ups and Downs of the Water Cycle" on page 127.

Tree Pattern

Use with "All Kinds of Kindness" on page 129, "Being Responsible Is 'Tree-mendous'" on page 130, and "Good Citizens of Long Ago" on page 130.

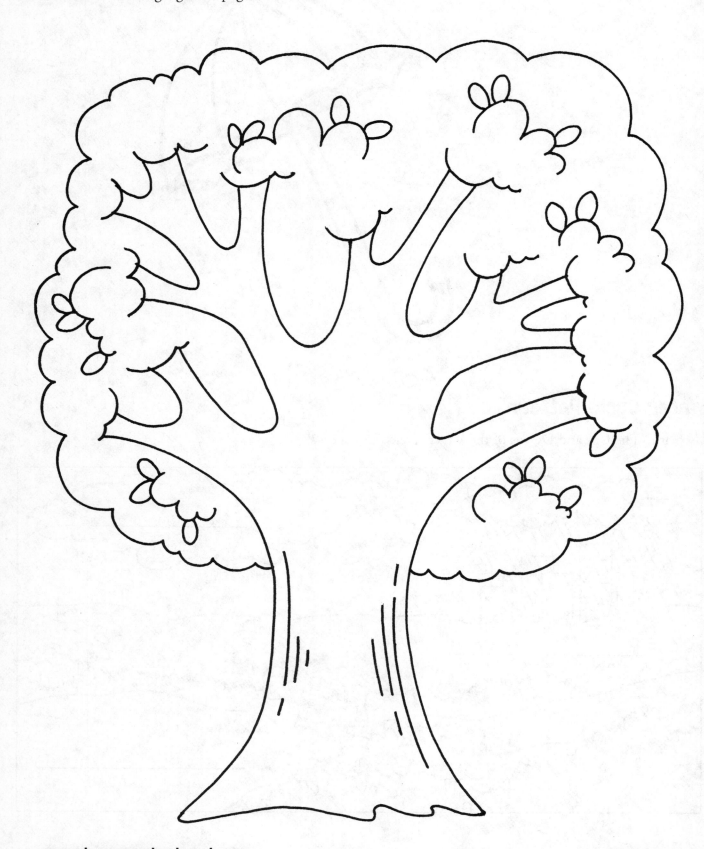

Apple Patterns

Use with "All Kinds of Kindness" on page 129 and "What's the Rule?" on page 131.

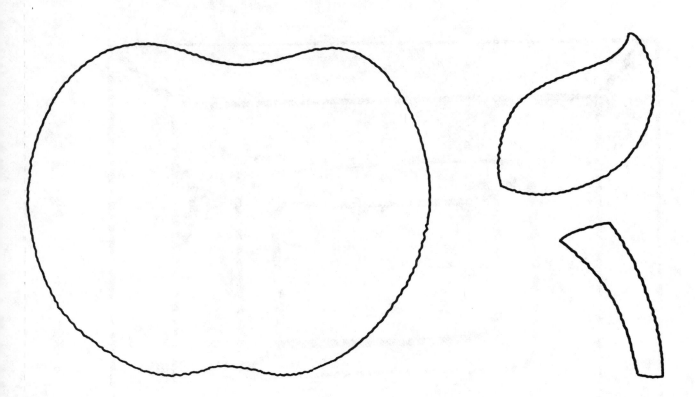

Leaf Pattern

Use with "Being Responsible Is 'Tree-mendous'" on page 130.

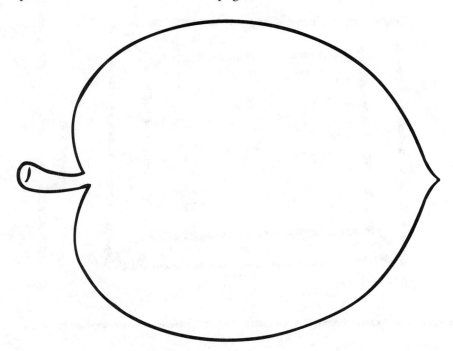

Door Pattern

Use with "Open the Door to the Past" on page 132.

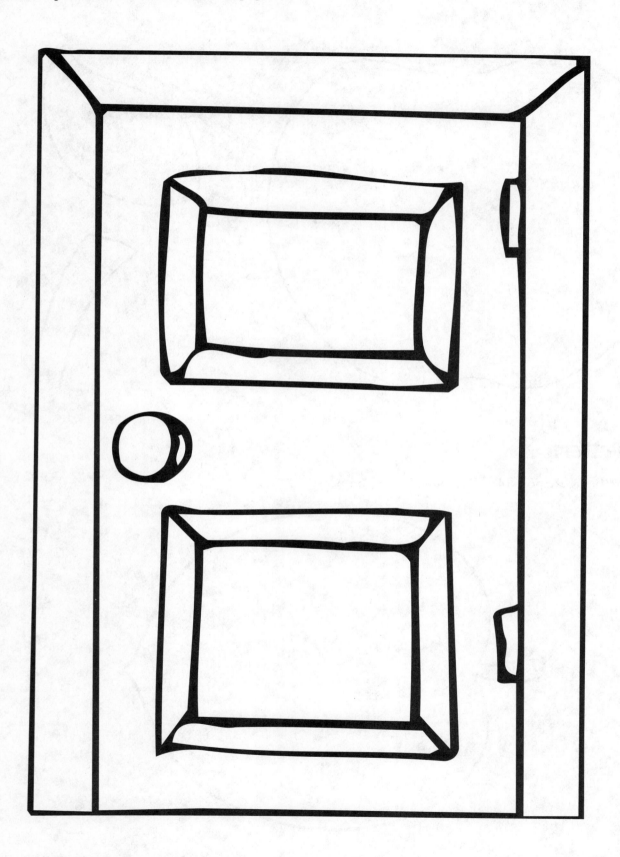

Photo Frame Pattern

Use with "People in Our School Community" on page 133 and "Picture This" on page 134.

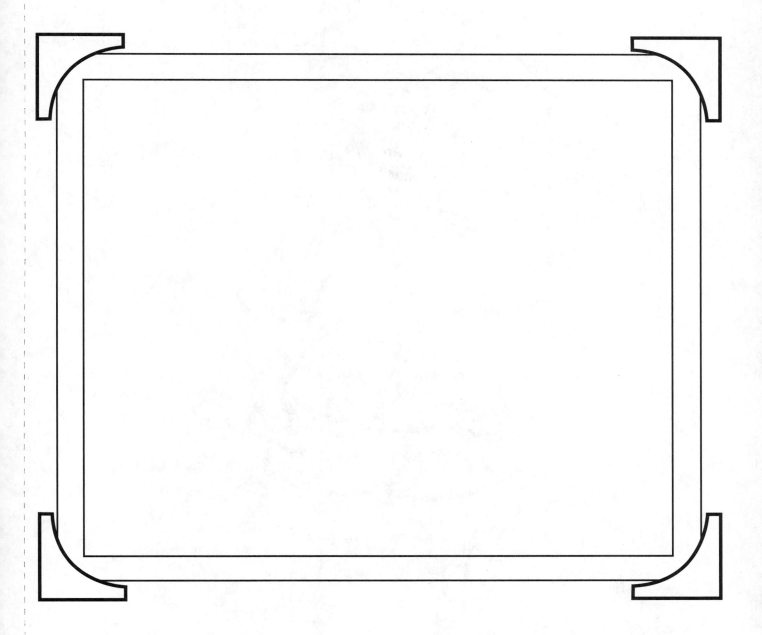

Man with Camera Pattern

Use with "Picture Perfect Communities" on page 133.

Mailbox Pattern

Use with "Addresses Are Important" on page 134.

Community Helper Picture Cards

Use with "Picture This" on page 134, "It's Off to Work We Go!" on page 136, "Serve Up the Goods" on page 136, "Help the Helpers" on page 137, and "We're Patrolling for Good Workers" on page 137.

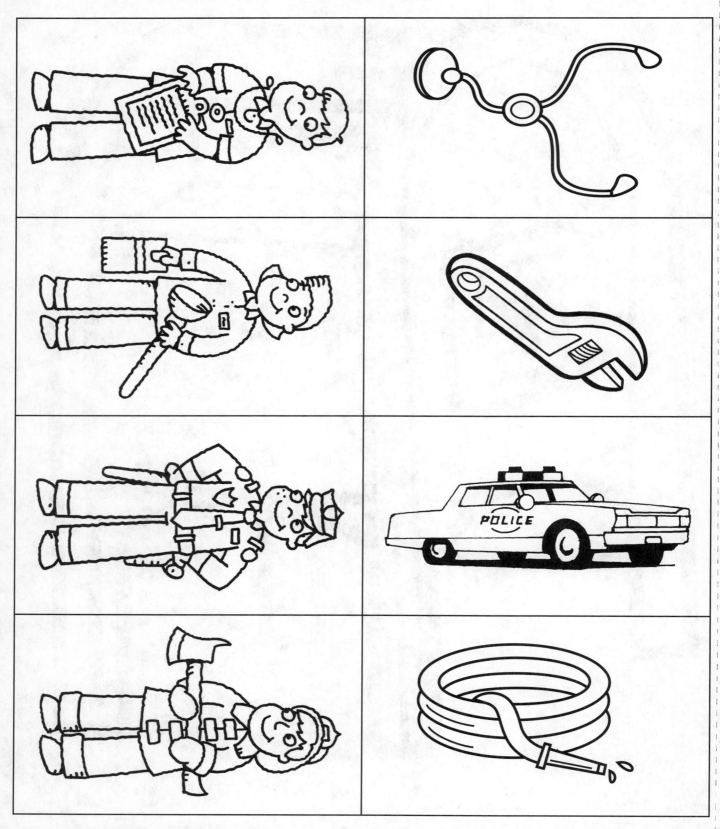

Community Helper Picture Cards (continued)

Use with "Picture This" on page 134, "It's Off to Work We Go" on page 136, "Serve Up the Goods" on page 136, and "Help the Helpers" on page 137.

Store Pattern

Use with "The Story of a Store" on page 135.

Owl Pattern

Use with "Be Wise—Follow These School Rules" on page 138, "Whooo Are the Leaders in This Town?" on page 139, "Wise Owls Use Dictionaries" on page 140, "Give a Hoot for the Environment!" on page 140, and "A Wise Owl Feathers Its Nest" on page 140.

Owl Parts Patterns

Use with "Be Wise—Follow These School Rules" on page 138.

Dictionary Pattern

Use with "Wise Owls Use Dictionaries" on page 140.

Town Pattern

Use with "Our Eyes Are on the Leaders" on page 139.

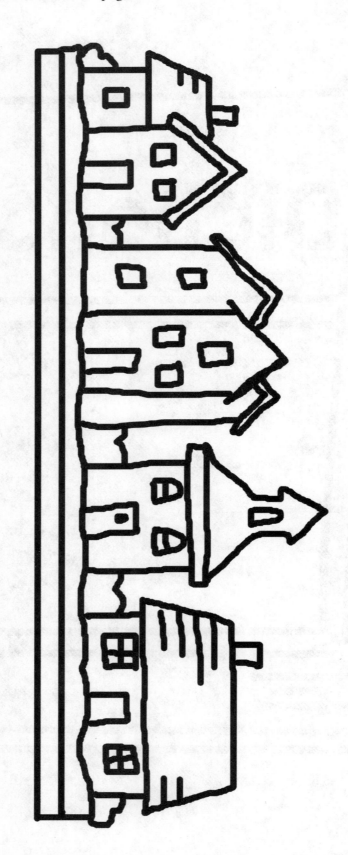

United States Map Pattern

Use with "Our Eyes Are on the Leaders" on page 139.

Sandwich Pattern

Use with "A 'Heart-y' Hero Sandwich" on page 142, "Sharing Sandwiches" on page 143, and "Serve Up a Sediment Sandwich" on page 143.

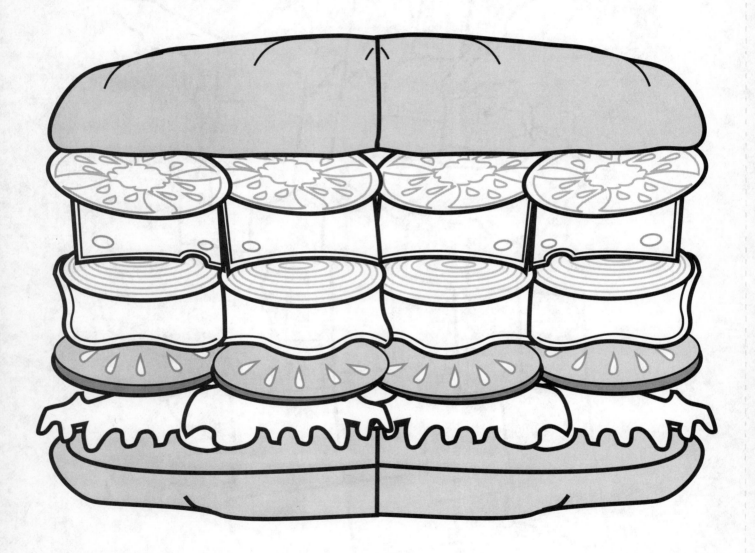

Heart Pattern

Use with "A 'Heart-y' Hero Sandwich" on page 142.

www.harcourtschoolsupply.com
243

Pattern
Bulletin Boards, SV 1-4190-1884-1

Continents Map Pattern

Use with "One If by Land, and Two If by Sea" on page 144, "High and Wide—Long and Far" on page 146, and "By the Clean Sea" on page 146.

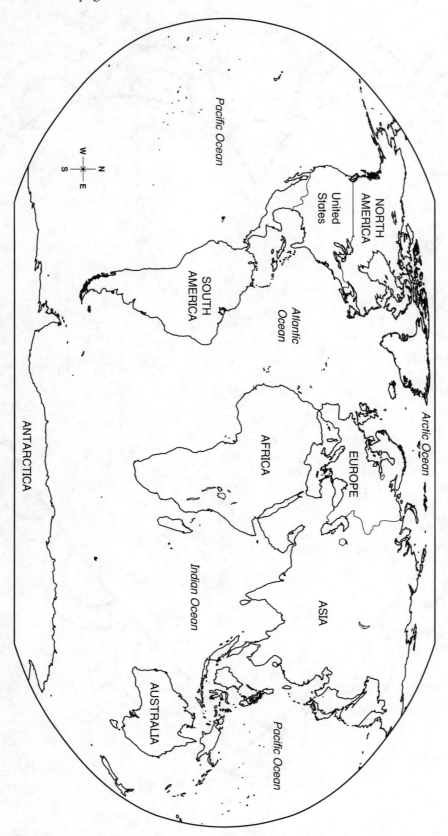

U.S. Landform and Bodies of Water Map Pattern

Use with "Where Will You Live?" on page 145 and "Capital Places We Know" on page 146.

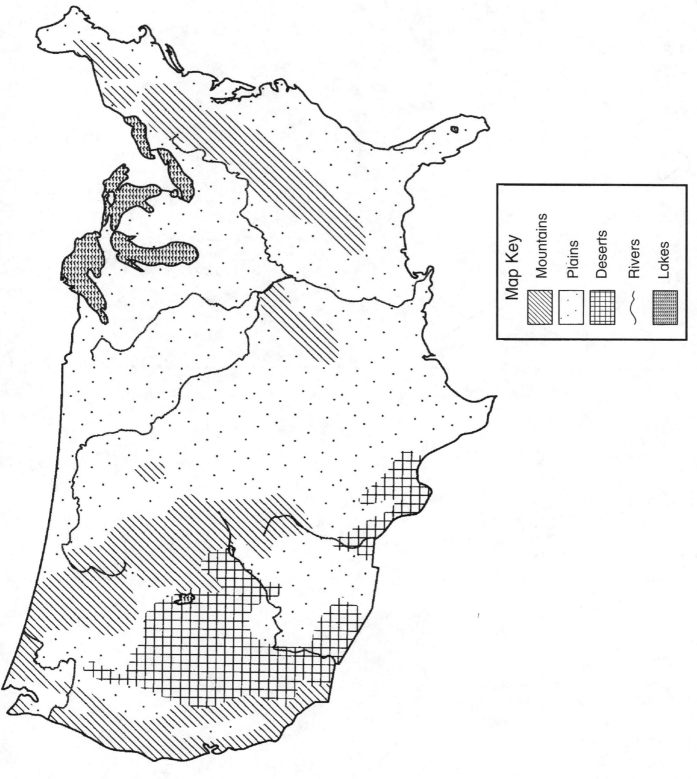

Map Key

Mountains
Plains
Deserts
Rivers
Lakes

Folded House Pattern

Use with "Building Communities" on page 145, "'House' Your Town?" on page 147, "A 'Fair-ly' Fun Day" on page 148, and "At Home with the ABCs" on page 149.

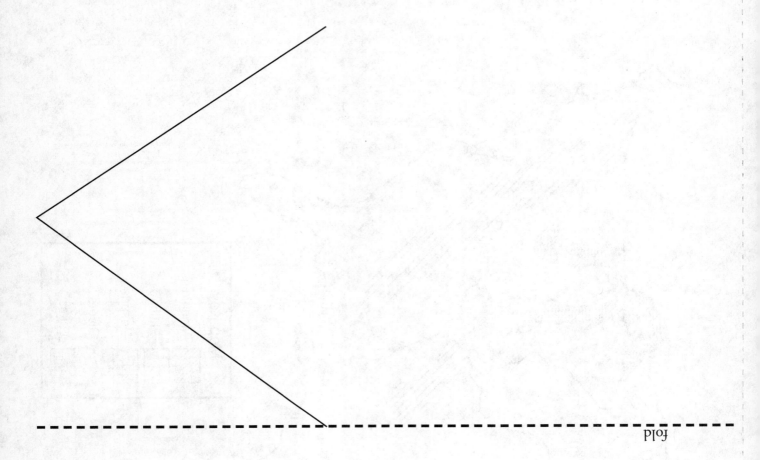

fold

Town Buildings Patterns

Use with "'House' Your Town?" on page 147, "Me on the Map!" on page 148, and "A Road Map for Good Behavior" on page 149.

Bulletin Boards, SV 1-4190-1884-1

Paper Doll Pattern

Use with "Safe in the Community" on page 122, "Me on the Map!" on page 148, and "Where Will You Live?" on page 145.

Pattern
Bulletin Boards, SV 1-4190-1884-1

Fair Grid Map Pattern

Use with "A 'Fair-ly' Fun Day!" on page 148 and "A Fair Way to Spend Money" on page 149.

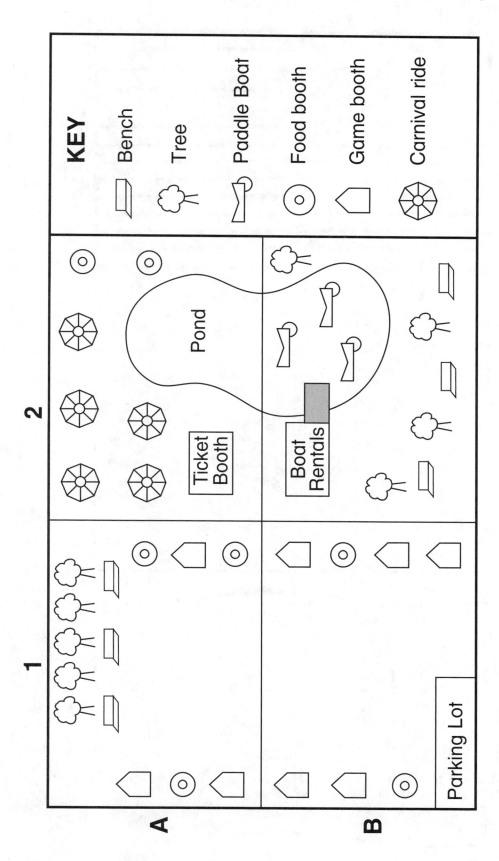

Flag Patterns

Use with "Be Proud of Your Flag" on page 150, "Symbolic Sentences" on page 152, and "Uncle Sam Wants You to Be a Good Worker" on page 152.

White House Pattern

Use with "Measure the White House" on page 152 and "Symbolic Sentences" on page 152.

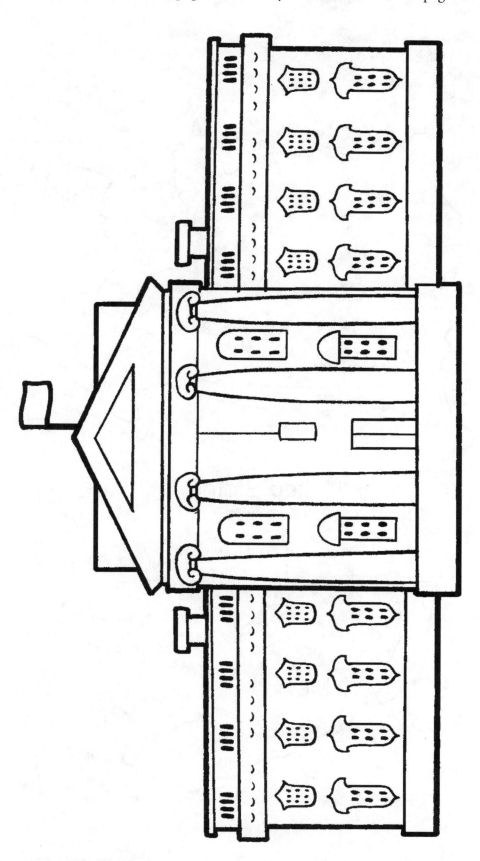

North America Map Pattern

Use with "Be Proud of Your Flag" on page 150.

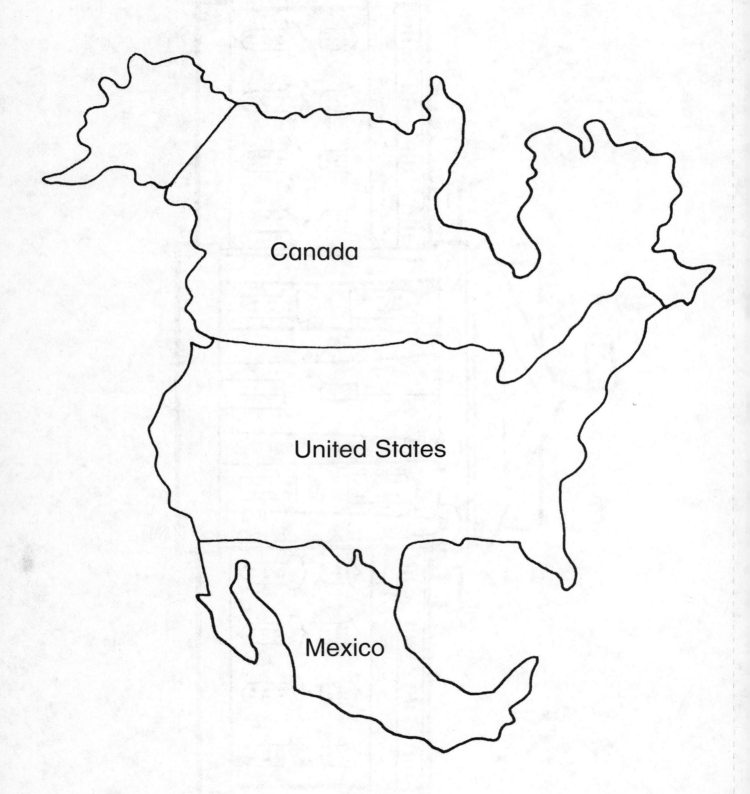

Canada

United States

Mexico

American Symbol Patterns

Use with "The Flip of a Coin" on page 151, "Uncle Sam Wants You to Be a Good Worker" on page 152, and "Symbolic Sentences" on page 152.

Pattern Index